STUDENT PARENT

STUDENT PARENT

THE FIGHT FOR FAMILIES, THE COST OF POVERTY, AND THE POWER OF COLLEGE

Nicole Lynn Lewis

BEACON PRESS
BOSTON

BEACON PRESS
24 Farnsworth Street
Boston, Massachusetts
www.beacon.org

Beacon Press books
are published under the auspices of
the Unitarian Universalist Association of Congregations.

Printed in the United States of America

29 28 27 26 8 7 6 5 4 3 2 1

This book is printed on acid-free paper that meets the uncoated paper ANSI/NISO specifications for permanence as revised in 1992.

Text design and composition by Kim Arney

Library of Congress Cataloguing-in-Publication Data is available for this title.
Hardcover ISBN: 978-0-8070-1757-9
E-book ISBN: 978-0-8070-1758-6
Audiobook: 978-0-8070-2217-7

The authorized representative in the EU for product safety and compliance is Easy Access System Europe 16879218, Mustamäe tee 50, 10621 Tallinn, Estonia: http://beacon.org/eu-contact.

This book is dedicated to Nancy, for teaching me the profound artistry of motherhood, to Nerissa, Naya, Donte Jr., Drew, and Devin, for instructing me in the truest meaning of love, without measure, and to the mothers and fathers who silently take care of us all. You are worthy and deserving of rest and abundance.

Well, when I think of the American dream, I think of exclusivity, to be quite honest with you. I think that dream, just like the Foundation of America, was only held out to a few, and it was only meant for a few.

—GLORIA NAYLOR

CONTENTS

CHAPTER 1

PROXIMITY AND THE CASSEROLE MINISTRY

The most disturbing circumstances can be bound in a meticulously sealed manila envelope, the pages neatly assembled, a paper clip carefully placed in the top right-hand corner, every question answered, every checkbox marked.

This is how it arrived. Back in 2010, the very first application to Generation Hope's Scholar Program came from Tatiana, a Virginia high school senior planning to start college in the fall. Her application described a smart young Latina who had made the honor roll in her junior and senior years and had already applied to Northern Virginia Community College with the hope of one day earning a bachelor's degree and becoming a nurse. She provided all of the required documents—an essay on the most significant obstacle she had overcome, transcripts, names and email addresses of three references—and mailed everything well before the deadline. The fact that Tatiana was also a young mother was not surprising; we had designed the Scholar Program to provide critical, wraparound support to teen parents in college. But when I scanned the application, a single date stood out, blurring everything else. A date that even I wasn't prepared for. Tatiana had given birth to her son at *twelve years old*.

During the previous year, a small group of us, board members and volunteers, had spent late nights over sushi and Starbucks conceptualizing and building our programming, based on my own experience as a young mother in college, our understanding of the teen parenting and teen pregnancy fields, and best practices from mentoring and youth-serving organizations. We imagined who our students would be, tried to anticipate their various needs, and baked those supports into our programming. We plotted out our logic model, defining how our intended impact and goals—ultimately, more young parents earning college degrees—connected to our activities and how we would measure success. We secured donated space from the University of the District of Columbia Community College and invited more than two hundred people from the area to a kickoff event to share the news that Generation Hope was ready to serve young parents who wanted to become college graduates. Then, we waited for applications.

Tatiana's manila envelope thrust me—all of us—very quickly into the realities of this work. Our introduction to the trauma, challenges, and complexities of families, parenting, racism, oppression, and poverty would come abruptly. We wouldn't be able to embark on this journey with the notion that any of it would be easy. This wouldn't be the ivory tower of higher education found in movies and fancy brochures—students lounging in hammocks or strolling across lush green campuses or gathered around beer kegs until dawn. Instead, there would be nights when our students' traumas disturbed our sleep and days when we'd have to remind each other, sometimes through tears, not to blame ourselves for things beyond our control. Generation Hope would sit at the nexus of struggle and promise, in the middle of hard things and incredible possibilities. Tatiana's application arrived as both a warning and a test. A warning that this work, while rewarding in ways that we couldn't imagine or even hope, would also be onerous and draining, even for seasoned youth professionals. A test to see if we were prepared to embrace and support *all students*, not just the ones who fit into neat little boxes.

On the day Tatiana's application arrived, questions traveled with me home from the office along the long tree-lined stretch of Baltimore-Washington Parkway just outside of DC: *What happened to her? What kind of life had she lived?* Pregnancy among ten- to twelve-year-olds is not typical, but half of women who have had sex by age eleven report that it was forced, and those who report otherwise were likely living through painful and confining childhoods.[1] Tatiana's story offered one of the most disturbing examples of a reality described so accurately by the World Health Organization: "While sexual activity among adolescents is to be expected because it is a normal part of human development, it often occurs in a broader context of structural and ideological inequality and power."[2] Without knowing all of Tatiana's story, I could guess it was laced with inequity and powerlessness, intricate patterns that would emerge in the lives of so many of the young people I would work with. This stuck with me even after I turned the key to our baby blue townhouse, nestled in a quiet Maryland cul-de-sac, and walked up the first flight of stairs to find my own eleven-year-old daughter, Nerissa, sitting at the kitchen table, doing her homework, throwing me a braces-lined smile over her shoulder.

Just a year earlier, I started Generation Hope in the basement of that townhouse with a clear premise: all families, including young families, deserve to thrive, and if we surround teen mothers and fathers who want to go to college with the financial and emotional resources that they deserve, we will see them succeed. More broadly, getting postsecondary credentials into the hands of more young parents could make a significant impact on poverty, housing, child hunger, and health disparities—it could help put an end to families struggling unnecessarily to survive. Fifty-two percent of all mothers on welfare in the US became parents as a teenager; despite federal and state welfare-to-work policies, they were never able to overcome the countless obstacles to accessing education and opportunity that they faced *before* their teen pregnancy and the many challenges that came after their child was born.[3]

Even without knowing the statistics at the time, I recognized that these policies were immensely flawed, that parents were capable and motivated to succeed, and that my own experience as a young mother in college gave me a springboard to plot an alternative, more effective way to stability and prosperity for families.

I graduated from William & Mary in Williamsburg, Virginia, in 2003, seven years before starting Generation Hope and five years after seeing two pink lines on a pregnancy test during my senior year of high school. On my graduation day, which also happened to be Mother's Day, Nerissa's tiny hand alternated between curling around my index finger and clutching my black gown while we walked across the stage to receive my diploma. It was an achievement we struggled to together—in a tangled symphony of sleepless nights, dean's lists, WIC benefits (the Special Supplemental Nutrition Program for Women, Infants, and Children), an honors thesis, and all the other daily contradictions of being a young, single Black mother attending one of the nation's "Public Ivies." Our difficult journey lit a tiny spark inside of me to make our story of triumph more commonplace, and a single statistic—fewer than 2 percent of teen mothers earn their degree before age thirty—ignited the fire.[4] It was clear to me that a postsecondary education could be a powerful economic force for young parents and their children—and for all families.

But in launching this work, I was contending with two formidable facts: regardless of how clear this was to me, creating college pathways for young mothers and fathers—the majority of whom are people of color living in poverty—was an unpopular solution, and falsehoods are easier to process and deal with than realities.

Today, 37.9 million Americans are living below the poverty line,[5] defined as $30,000 a year for a family of four.[6] That's about 11.6 percent of the population. You would have to fill Michigan Stadium, the largest football stadium in the US, more than 350 times to hold all of the people in America who the government identifies as poor.[7] In reality, the official number of people who struggle to pay rent every month or to find enough food to make it through a day is much larger. An outdated government measure of the poverty line means the actual number of families whose lives are shaped and scarred by scarcity is far higher.[8] About half of all US families can't pay their bills, subjected to a grueling daily exercise of survival.[9] It's an exertion I knew well as a young mother in college, my thoughts routinely consumed with creative calculations for ensuring that Nerissa was fed, clothed, and had a bed to sleep in for the next twenty-four hours.

Despite being ranked the world's richest nation in terms of gross domestic product (GDP),[10] the United States consistently earns the distinction of having one of the highest child poverty rates.[11] The reasons so many American families are living in poverty are multifaceted and numerous: it's incredibly expensive to raise children, and most costly for those with the fewest resources; current economic policies fail to meet families' basic needs and disincentivize educational pursuits that could lead to higher earnings; income inequality has been allowed to grow dramatically since the 1970s, helped in part by a federal minimum wage frozen for more than a decade; and workforce racism, sexism, and discrimination keep people of color, especially Black, Hispanic, and Indigenous women, disproportionately represented in jobs with low pay and inadequate benefits.[12] In short, our systems and structures keep economic power in the hands of the few while we blame those who live in poverty for not securing it.

Single mothers of color, who are the most likely people to be living in poverty with their children, find economic power especially hard to reach, leaving them to navigate low wages and no access to paid leave and quality, consistent childcare.[13] Without these basic protections, working full-time—or at all—can feel impossible, never mind enrolling, or staying enrolled, in college. Nearly 30 percent of single mothers live in poverty with their children compared to just 6 percent of married couples.[14] Political rhetoric that can be traced back to President Ronald Reagan's "welfare queen" trope, which played on the racial resentment of white Americans and described welfare as single Black mothers looking to game the system, helped to perpetuate the lie that poverty is a result of individual choices rather than structural failings. In reality, as Matthew Desmond writes in *Poverty, by America*, "Choosing to have a child outside of marriage may be an individual choice, but condemning many of those parents and their children to a life of poverty is a societal one."[15]

My son's preschool is housed within an Episcopal church, and in the lobby where the sign-out sheets are displayed for parents, there is a station for the church's "casserole ministry." It's a stack of aluminum foil pans with a recipe taped inside each one along with directions for where to drop the warm, bubbling meal to feed a family in need. Several pans are taken from week to week, then the stack is replenished again. The popularity of the casserole ministry can be attributed to its convenience and ease, mirroring America's preferences when it comes to helping those in need. We are more likely to rally around solutions that focus on symptoms of our most pressing problems rather than their root causes.[16] Homeless services, food banks, crisis centers, and coat drives give people a palatable way of dealing with poverty. Providing a night in a shelter or a tasty casserole allows us to feel good about helping others who have fallen on hard times as a result of their own unfortunate individual choices like dropping out of school, selling drugs, or having a baby out of wedlock.

While basic-needs organizations are vital to our social ecosystem, alone, they don't create lasting change. A winter coat or back-to-school supplies don't combat the underlying reasons that students of color are more likely to drop out of school[17] or that people who sell drugs are often suffering from their own addictions[18] or that the policies *we* create, such as the 1996 welfare reform law that forced single moms to fend for themselves,[19] actually make it more difficult for them to provide for their families.[20] The casserole ministry allows us to stay in a distant comfort zone, ignoring the conditions that created food or housing insecurity in the first place, a dangerous illusion, according to Dr. Martin Luther King Jr., who said that philanthropy "must not cause the philanthropist to overlook the circumstances of economic injustice which make philanthropy necessary."[21] Generation Hope isn't the casserole ministry. Instead, it counters the idea that young parents live in poverty because of their own bad choices and amplifies America's long-standing practice of economic injustice that makes success and stability nearly impossible for families in poverty.

In launching Generation Hope, I had to overcome the fact that, like with most pressing social issues, much of what people know about teen pregnancy is rooted not in data but in rhetoric. The rhetoric tells us that teen pregnancy causes poverty, making it easier to blame young parents for their own plight and to withhold resources that could help them. But in reality, *poverty* causes teen pregnancy,[22] just as poverty causes mass incarceration,[23] high school dropouts,[24] illiteracy,[25] and more. Despite what we've been conditioned to believe, poverty is rarely an unfortunate consequence of bad choices and decisions but rather a constant state of literal and figurative starvation that millions of people have inherited from the generations before them. South African anti-apartheid leader Nelson Mandela described poverty as a violation: "The very right to be human is denied every day to hundreds of millions of people as a result of poverty, the unavailability of basic necessities such as food, jobs, water and shelter, education, health care and a healthy environment."[26]

About eleven million children—one in seven children in the US—are poor,[27] and more than 70 percent of them are children of color.[28] These young people are growing up in communities that have been historically starved of opportunities, good schools, family-sustaining wages, basic needs such as housing, food, and healthcare, and so much more—conditions that contribute to higher teen birth rates.[29] Instead of investing in structural reforms that would address generational poverty and oppression and help to prevent teen pregnancies and other overwhelming setbacks for these communities, we address surface issues and villainize the people who are most impacted.

The villains in the story of teen pregnancy, single motherhood, poverty, hunger, and homelessness are typically Black and Brown people and most often young women. They are likely to be living in communities still grappling with the day-to-day ripple effects of genocide, slavery, and oppression dating back to the founding of America. American Indian/Alaska Native teen girls have the highest teen birth rates, almost three times that of white teen girls, followed by Black and Hispanic/Latina teen girls, whose teen birth rate is more than two times that of white teen girls.[30] Identifying their pregnancy as the single event that sent them on a downward spiral to poverty overlooks the many challenges that come with growing up Indigenous, Black, or Latino in America. They were navigating a world of harsh inequities with far-reaching impacts long before their pregnancies. Having a child merely exacerbates these challenges and makes economic mobility even more illusory.

For more than fifteen years, Generation Hope has done this work, walking alongside teen mothers and fathers in their pursuit of an associate's or bachelor's degree. Our students, who graduate at a rate on par with the national average for all college students whether they're parenting or not, have proven with every degree earned that they are not the problem, *our systems* are the problem. Whether they are experiencing failures in healthcare, K–12, or human services systems, individuals who don't meet the criteria for what is deemed "good" and "right" are not given the resources or opportunities to thrive. Young parents, who are more likely to be Black, Hispanic/Latino, and Indigenous, rarely meet these criteria; parents of any age who are living in poverty or who don't have a legacy of higher education in their families rarely meet these criteria. As an organization, we realized several years ago that we had to create the conditions for all families to thrive—that our work with young parents gives us the insight and perspective to champion systemic change in an authentic way that disrupts the criteria and the systems that give them power.

This work frequently puts me in conversations about economic mobility at events hosted by foundations, educational institutions, nonprofits, think tanks, or companies. The problem everyone is trying to solve is the same: too many people are living in poverty, and the numbers aren't improving. The wealth gap between America's richest and poorer families more than doubled in the past thirty years. Despite a greater awareness of racial disparities, the income gap between Black and white Americans remains, meaning there is far too much dialogue about racism and nowhere near enough action.[31] The COVID-19 pandemic that engulfed the globe beginning in 2020 devastated families already on the fringes, particularly Black, Hispanic/Latino, and Indigenous families, and, more specifically, Black and Brown mothers. Why these families were hit hardest is no mystery. Past and present exclusion from economic and social mobility made them particularly vulnerable to the financial and health-related impacts of COVID. At the same time, an unanticipated outcome of the pain and suffering caused by the pandemic has been a renewed—and, at times, entirely new—determination to fix it.

The answer in these conversations is almost always workforce development—vocational programs that provide workers with job training, certificates, and opportunities to upskill, aligned with the economy's labor needs. Workforce development emerged as a federal initiative in the nineteenth century to create economic stability and security for individuals, communities, and the nation. Today, workforce development boards, programs, and organizations make up an ecosystem to close the skills gap and help individuals experience economic mobility. Historically, the workforce development field, like many public policies, has systematically excluded people of color. When President Barack Obama signed the Workforce Innovation and Opportunity Act (WIOA) in 2014, it marked a significant shift toward more intentional inclusion of marginalized populations in workforce and adult education programs.[32] While innovative efforts are emerging under the workforce development umbrella, funding for training workers is desperately needed. According to the National Skills Coalition, workforce development spending has dropped by two-thirds over the last four decades while the workforce has grown by 50 percent.[33] For these and other reasons, *work* is repeatedly cited as the solution, with the idea that putting individuals into jobs is the best way to solve the country's poverty problem.

Getting people into jobs is important, but it's just a piece of the puzzle. Which jobs people move into, how much they get paid, and whether those jobs give them access to promotions, healthcare, sick leave, and money for childcare, these are the important factors that determine the trajectory of an individual and their family.

In these discussions, I'm often the lone person around the virtual or physical table saying a word rarely associated with moms and dads living in poverty: *college*. That's because despite the fact that workforce development includes postsecondary opportunities, few people consider college a realistic option for parents struggling to create a better life for their families, especially Black and Brown parents. The omission of higher education as a pathway for family success and stability is both a deafening and silent judgment about who is deserving, who is worthy, and who is likely to succeed. A single Latina mother of three experiencing housing instability should be cleaning hotel rooms rather than pursuing a passion for computer engineering at her local community college, even if that path means never owning a home or even being able to pay her monthly bills. The best she can and *should* hope for is a workforce training program to become a certified nursing assistant earning $30,000 a year. While a degree would lead to higher earnings and benefits like healthcare and sick leave, it's a far-flung fantasy for a domestic worker with a high school diploma. Any effort to support her college dreams would be a waste of time and resources.

This ugly sentiment is waiting for me in almost every room I enter when I speak to others about Generation Hope. Whether it's a small church group on a Sunday evening or a large gathering of executives at a weekday retreat, someone will ask why we don't focus on helping teen parents earn certificates in trades like cosmetology or auto mechanics instead of college degrees. The sentiment also finds its way into conversations with some funders that focus their philanthropic dollars on training low-income, unemployed, and underemployed people for better-paying jobs. When I talk about Generation Hope sharing the goal of getting underserved populations into family-sustaining careers, but through higher education, they shift in their seats. They don't consider college a part of their job strategy. This sentiment reveals a ceiling that we, consciously or not, place on the aspirations of those experiencing poverty. As the gatekeepers of resources and opportunity, we believe *we* should define what *their* success looks like. We believe we know what's best for these families. They shouldn't have the luxury of choosing their own path, and certainly not if that path is to a college degree.

When I watch my children chase after bubbles or roast marshmallows around our firepit under the towering oak and maple trees that crowd our backyard, I'm reminded how flawed any blueprint for moving marginalized populations into family-sustaining careers is if it doesn't include higher education. My degrees have unlocked a life for our family that I never thought possible as a young mother who often went to bed hungry. College is the cornerstone of how high-income families in America secure economic stability and success for their children. Their path to higher education starts early with access to high-quality preschool, stellar public (and private) K–12 schools, extra tutoring, costly college prep programs, training for standardized tests, and countless other strategic investments in their children's futures.

More than 80 percent of high school seniors from wealthier families immediately enroll in college compared to 67 percent of high school seniors from low-income families,[34] and those under-resourced students who do enroll are seven times less likely to earn a bachelor's degree by age twenty-four than their higher-income peers.[35] Racism, discrimination, and oppression make the road to college for families with lower income hard to even find. For example, more than one in ten children in the US live in neighborhoods with concentrated poverty and under-resourced schools.[36] These children, more likely to be children of color, often go to school with nothing in their bellies, worrying whether Mom or Dad or Grandma will be able to pay rent this month, leaving little room for thoughts about life after high school.

There are—and have been—herculean efforts to get these students into and through college. College completion programs that infuse the necessary resources and supports into the lives of students from under-resourced communities provide proof points for policymakers to create sweeping change. But two key populations are usually missing from programmatic efforts to increase college access and completion: 1) the millions of current students who are raising children and 2) the millions of parents who might enroll in college if they believed it was a place where they could succeed. Those who stand to benefit most from a postsecondary credential, an education that would have generational impacts, are among the least likely to be considered or supported.

Similarly, policymakers have been slow to recognize college as a viable pathway for moving families out of poverty. For a single father who is working the midnight shift as a janitor but wants to one day design buildings of his own, the focus remains on just keeping him employed. Proponents of these deficient policies fall back on an unremitting question to justify their position: "Is college even worth it?" We wouldn't pose this question to the child of a senator or other member of Congress, but we ask it regularly when talking about those who don't meet our narrow definition for who deserves a degree. And in asking it, we ignore the data on the clear return on investment of a postsecondary credential: the median salary for workers with high school diplomas is $38,792 compared to the median salary for workers with bachelor's degrees of $64,896.[37] In our own research at Generation Hope, we found that annual earnings *more than doubled* for young parents after graduating from college.[38] Will a college degree make that much of a difference for that single father and his little ones? The answer is a resounding yes. Over the course of his lifetime, he could earn hundreds of thousands of dollars more, thanks to his degree.

Parents like this father are everywhere, working at our favorite coffee shop or restaurant, cleaning our offices, answering phones. Many have attempted college at some point, only to be pushed to the margins by the demands of parenting, where the combined costs of raising children and pursuing a degree are crippling. More than thirty million Americans have attended college but never earned a degree. Despite the fact that 35 percent of them are parents of at least one dependent child, this group is rarely mentioned in the movement to reengage adult learners in higher education.[39] We don't picture parents when we think about the average college student, not because they aren't in college classrooms, but because we've decided they don't belong there.

Who we are today and who and what we prioritize can be traced back to how we began. The origins of higher education in this country can tell us why mothers and fathers have been historically and systemically excluded from the benefits of a college degree. On Sunday, August 13, 1786, one of America's founding fathers, Thomas Jefferson, wrote to his mentor, George Wythe, from Paris, where he was serving as Benjamin Franklin's successor as US minister. In his letter, Jefferson emphasized his belief that the success of the new country trying to establish itself depended on a system of broad, free, public education:

> I think by far the most important bill in our whole code is that for the diffusion of knowlege [*sic*] among the people. no other sure foundation can be devised for the preservation of freedom, and happiness.[40]

A little over thirty years later, Jefferson's beliefs would translate into action when he founded the University of Virginia, a public institution guided by the ideals of "collaboration and enlightenment."[41] Enslaved people helped to build the university when construction began in 1817. They represented a significant number of the workers who tended the grounds, prepared meals, cleaned rooms and facilities, and stocked supplies, but it would take more than 130 years for the first Black student, Gregory H. Swanson, to be admitted, on September 15, 1950. Women were similarly excluded from the collaboration and enlightenment that the institution provided. It wasn't until the fall of 1920 that seventeen women were allowed to enroll.

Jefferson's vision of a broad public education served a narrowly defined student—the affluent white man. The founding fathers intended for these men to be America's leaders, and therefore, they would need a college education. Nothing about the origins of our higher education system and its exclusions were accidental. US higher education historian Frederick Rudolph writes, "In the beginning, higher education in America would be governed less by accident than by certain purpose, less by impulse than by design."[42] And Craig Steven Wilder, historian and author of *Ebony & Ivy*, gives us more insight into the specific design: "Every college that survived the American Revolutionary War did so by attaching itself to the slave economies of the Atlantic world. It's those economies that sustained them. Slavery wasn't just an aspect of their early history—slavery decided which colleges would survive."[43] The nine early colonial colleges—Harvard, William & Mary, Yale, New Jersey, King's, Philadelphia, Rhode Island, Queen's, and Dartmouth—were built on the backs of enslaved people and designed to serve white men. These exclusions were subsequently baked into the DNA of the higher education system that we know today and influenced the proliferation of institutions that would follow. Today, 75 percent of the students enrolled at the 468 best-funded and most selective four-year institutions in this country are white.[44] On these campuses, like many campuses, you are more likely to find people of color tending to the grounds, preparing meals, cleaning rooms and facilities, and stocking supplies than sitting in the classrooms.

Before he founded the University of Virginia, Thomas Jefferson was a student at William & Mary—the same school I would attend more than two hundred years later as a young Black mother. The same school that owned and sold enslaved people and where the first women to walk its grounds were enslaved.[45] I, along with millions of other parenting students, was an impossibility as far as Jefferson and the other founding fathers were concerned, and the structures, systems, traditions, and norms there reinforced that notion. It often felt like the whole world was moving around me in a flurry of classes and studying and social life with little understanding or recognition of who I was. My days revolved around Nerissa, who wasn't even three months old when I started my freshman year, getting her to daycare, paying rent, and praying we'd have enough food to last us through the week. At night, I stayed up until early morning finishing my reading and papers, and I'd wake up a few hours later to start the day again, trying to hold us together under the pressure of it all.

My experience mirrors the experiences of America's student parent population—mothers and fathers who are currently enrolled in undergraduate programs across the country. Nearly five million parents attend US colleges and universities—roughly one in five students—but they fall off the radar of most people working in higher education and are even more invisible in the economic mobility movement. These students are highly motivated—on average they earn higher GPAs than students without children[46]—but they are ten times less likely to earn a bachelor's degree within five years[47] because of the many hurdles they face and the dearth of resources. Student parents are integral to the problems we're trying to solve—poverty, racial equity, future of work, economic recovery, education—but our inability to *see* them makes these problems bigger.

I recently spoke at a conference in Atlanta before a group of higher education leaders working in historically Black colleges across the country. The conference was held at a large Marriott Hotel. Behind the scenes was an intricate operation of hundreds of hotel employees serving lunch, directing guests, cleaning rooms, refilling beverage stations. They were trained to be invisible, to get their jobs done without disrupting events or disturbing guests. The backstage area was right in front of the kitchen door, and as I waited for my turn to take the stage, I watched dozens of workers, mostly Black, Hispanic, and Latino, dressed in perfectly ironed black and white uniforms, going in and out of the kitchen to ensure lunch plates were cleared and coffee cups were filled. The organizers had asked me to speak about student parents and the needed transformations across higher education. I realized that by sitting just outside of the kitchen, I had a front-row seat to a critically important insight. During my talk, I asked the audience to consider that their potential students were not just sitting in high school classrooms somewhere or taking campus tours, they were also right there, working in that hotel, unseen, many of them parents. Despite how close these workers were to the attendees, they might never be seen as college material.

This is our proximity problem. We keep families in poverty close enough to clear our plates and fill our coffee cups but far enough from transformational opportunities that could build their wealth and power. Like the Marriott employees working a college success event, this is not a *physical* proximity problem. Parents are already close to—and already in—educational spaces. Young mothers and fathers are sitting *in* high school classrooms where teachers and counselors should be helping them graduate and talking to them about college. Parents of all ages are driving Ubers and pulling the night shifts in factories *near* college campuses. You can also find them working behind the counters in the dining halls or at the ticket office at stadiums and performing arts buildings *on* campus. And they're even racing from one college building to another, trying to get to their next class on time, with little support or validation, forced to leave their full identities as caregivers at the door.

Instead, the proximity issue is relative. Parents with low income are so far from postsecondary opportunities and achievements because of their intersecting identities of being under-resourced individuals, students of color, first-generation college students, and working students, their parenting responsibilities further relegating them to the fringes. They're not included in conversations around equity and student success because we don't even factor them into the equation.

We condemn people in poverty for not pursuing an education, but in order to strive for something, you need at least a small hope that it's within your grasp. When we shut parents out of educational opportunities, ignore their needs, devalue their experiences, treat them as unworthy, withhold support and resources, we make it hard for them to feel like college is possible. And if they even make it *into* college, is it realistic to think that they will make it *through* college? More than half of all student parents stop out of college, or temporarily leave their studies, before earning their degree. The financial costs, time demands, and the stigma of not belonging can be overwhelming.[48] Although many of these students were systematically shut out of higher education long before becoming parents, the erosion of family-friendly policies in the US has made the path out of poverty—and the hope of a better future for their children—incredibly bleak. Increasing the minimum wage, reinstating and expanding the Child Tax Credit, and establishing universal pre-K would provide immediate relief for mothers and fathers. Free college programs, ongoing emergency aid grants to students, and funding to make colleges more family friendly could help carve a path to college success.

These investments would require us to see *all* families as worthy, deserving, and capable of succeeding. Instead, we decry parents and children in poverty, and our systems and processes perpetuate superficial solutions—never penetrating the thick fortified layers of oppression at the core of our issues. They feed off of rhetoric and misinformation that keep us from hitting the mark and their mechanics overlook and omit the people who should benefit, regardless of how obvious they should be. All of this can feel too enormous and unruly to change, but systems are malleable. James Clear, author of *Atomic Habits*, helps people change simple daily behaviors from negative to positive to achieve better overall results. Clear writes, "Behind every system of actions is a system of beliefs." On a scale larger than eating healthier or making it to the gym more often, Clear's take on what undergirds a system remains true. In the shadows of our inability to dismantle poverty sits a ruthless system of beliefs about these families. In 2001, National Public Radio, the Kaiser Family Foundation, and Harvard University's Kennedy School asked nearly two thousand Americans over the age of eighteen: "Which is the bigger cause of poverty today: that people are not doing enough to help themselves out of poverty, or that circumstances beyond their control cause them to be poor?" They found that more than 50 percent of Americans believe that lack of motivation is a major cause of poverty. Little progress will be made until we confront and challenge these beliefs, and establish new ways of thinking aligned with the results we want to see.

During the 2021 book tour for my memoir, *Pregnant Girl*, I talked to a group of about thirty teen mothers at a high school in San Francisco, California. After reading *Pregnant Girl*, they were armed with questions. Some asked about my turbulent relationship with my daughter's father because it reminded them of their own struggles to co-parent. Others wanted to see the long driveway that I describe in the book—a driveway that took me to a house I never thought I'd be able to afford when I was a young mother struggling to pay rent. We cried together, as we shared our collective experiences and dreams for the future. Toward the end, a mother bundled up in a bulky black jacket, her long dark hair pulled into a neat bun, raised her hand. In a quiet voice, after glancing at her teacher for reassurance, she asked, "Why are you so obsessed with college?" I laughed. I had heard versions of the question before, usually from people concerned that we're promoting college as the only route to economic security. But this was the first time I'd heard it asked so plainly, and the first time it came from a young parent.

Still, my answer was the same: "I'm not obsessed with college. I'm obsessed with you having *the choice* to go to college."

Tatiana, our very first applicant, who became a mother at twelve, didn't end up enrolling in our program at Generation Hope. Shortly after her interview, she declined her acceptance, saying she didn't think she needed mentoring support, a key component of our model. We'll never know why she didn't want a mentor, why she ultimately turned down the opportunity for us to help her reach her goals. It could have simply been because she didn't think she had the time, or it could have been much bigger than that. Perhaps the idea of having to build trust with someone given everything she had been through in her life was just too scary, too risky. Perhaps she wasn't ready to be a part of a program that celebrated and named the fact that she was a mother after being conditioned to hide it in shame. We'll never know, but I like to imagine that she enrolled at Northern Virginia Community College, earned her associate's degree, and went on to a four-year school, where she earned her bachelor's degree. I like to think she is caring for patients in a hospital somewhere, maybe even supervising other nurses. This is what I want to believe. I want to believe that even without Generation Hope, she had a choice in what her life would be like.

At the same time, I sit in the reality that for the vast majority of mothers and fathers experiencing poverty, choice is a luxury. College is out of reach. A long driveway is a daydream. And food on the table is a gamble each night. This reality calls us, each of us, to create a different and better world where people—regardless of their background, resources, race, or ethnicity and their ability to fit into neat little boxes or meet someone else's criteria—feel close enough to opportunities that they have power over their destinies and the ability to pursue them unencumbered and unbound. A world where we wrestle with the uncomfortable root causes of scarcity and suffering to effectively help others. A world that doesn't force people to hide the scars that we have caused but sees them, acknowledges them, and does the healing work. A world that doesn't ask us to be something we're not but sees us for who we are and values the richness of our experiences. What a world that would be.

CHAPTER 2

RACE AND TINY SPARKS

A tiny, apricot-colored spark is born from indiscernible carbon particles released into the flame. Fed by a simple piece of wood or slip of paper, it grows fuller, becoming something else, transforming into a blaze, a weapon even. Important revolutions and tragic massacres alike have begun with just a miniscule quiver of light, illuminating the restless faces of the small or massive crowd that surrounded it.

In the early morning hours of Wednesday, June 1, 1921, a small flicker would ignite what would become one of the worst racial terror attacks in US history, the Tulsa Race Massacre, destroying the neighborhood of Greenwood in Tulsa, Oklahoma. Home to ten thousand Black residents, Greenwood was a thriving district of commerce, culture, and life. Staples like Zulu Lounge, Isaac Evitt's small juke joint, where sorrowful, triumphant, and sultry blues swayed late into the night. Mount Zion Baptist Church, the city's largest Black church, where members spilled outside after the service on Sunday afternoons to greet one another with hearty handshakes and warm embraces. The Bell and Little Café, where on Thursday nights the Cajun and Creole spices from Susie Bell and Presley Little's famous smothered chicken beckoned the domestic workers with the night off. Greenwood, or "Black Wall Street," stood proudly against the backdrop of racial oppression, showing what *could be* for Black Americans. While technological progress and its byproducts in the US during the 1920s led to a surge in consumers and economic growth, discrimination, racist hierarchies, and systemic oppression kept the vast majority of Black Americans in poverty. Greenwood was not only a rarity, it was a dazzling gem; it was likely the wealthiest Black community in the country.[1]

The kindling for the fire took shape the day before in an elevator of the Drexel Building in downtown Tulsa—the perfect conditions to ignite the inferno that would follow. Out of that elevator came an accusation that a sexual assault occurred between a young Black man named Dick Rowland and a white woman who were inside. The next day, Rowland was arrested and jailed. A *Tulsa Tribune* front-page article, "Nab Negro for Attacking Girl in Elevator," sealed his fate and the fate of Greenwood by mobilizing a lynch mob. The 1920s not only brought an economic boom to the US; it also ushered in a resurgence of the Ku Klux Klan (KKK), a white supremacist terrorist group that had dropped off in popularity for decades. Along with other influences, the violent 1915 anti-Black film *The Birth of a Nation*, directed by Kentuckian D. W. Griffith, depicted the KKK as the hero of the Reconstruction South and revived interest and followers. By the mid-1920s, nearly four million Americans claimed Klan membership.[2] After the Tulsa Race Massacre, the Tulsa Klan numbered two thousand members, many of whom initiated the violence that ravaged Greenwood in 1921.[3]

The mob moved from house to house, building to building, consuming each structure with a fiery orange blaze. Public officials gave firearms and ammunition to white rioters. Rioters dragged Black residents from their homes and shot them in the streets. They stole jewelry and money. Greenwood residents tried to defend themselves, but they were outnumbered, and in the charcoal smoke-filled skies above, white pilots dropped dynamite from planes down onto the streets below. For twenty-four hours, the city burned. When the smoke cleared, thirty-five blocks were charred and melted, as many as three hundred were dead—many thrown into mass graves—more than eight hundred were injured, eight thousand to ten thousand were left homeless, and six thousand were detained at the Convention Hall and the fairgrounds in internment camps. Thomas James Sharp, corporate secretary of the Garfield Petroleum Company in Enid, Oklahoma, described the aftermath in a letter to his parents, buried among news about his newborn son and how well business was going: "I suppose you read all about the race riots in Tulsa a few weeks ago. It sure was some riot. I saw the remains of nigger town when I went over . . . and there wasn't as much as a stick of wood standing in a piece of land a mile square, and believe me you can build a lot of nigger houses in that much territory."[4]

More than one hundred years later, no one has ever been held accountable for the destruction or murders at any level of government, and most US history school curriculums omit or provide only a brief mention of the Tulsa Race Massacre. Even in Oklahoma, most residents never received a full lesson on the Tulsa Race Massacre or Black Wall Street in their K–12 education,[5] and now a state law, Oklahoma House Bill 1775, is banning concepts about race in public schools that could further threaten even a watered-down version of the facts. For students who receive a diluted account of this event, race relations are often identified as the root cause of the demise of Greenwood. While hatred for Black people fueled the fire, so did an intense fear and a perceived threat among neighboring white communities that Greenwood was amassing too much wealth.

The economic costs of the massacre were immense and generational. Property loss claims alone totaled $1.8 million—$27 million in today's dollars. All but one of these claims were denied by racist insurers.[6] But estimates on the total financial impact have continued to rise. Researchers in a 2018 article in the *American Journal of Economics and Sociology* wrote, "The additional loss of other assets, including cash, personal belongings, and commercial property, might bring the total to over $200 million." O. W. Gurley, a wealthy Black landowner commonly referred to as one of the founders of Greenwood, lost his entire fortune—nearly $158,000, or $2.3 million in today's dollars—in the violence. In addition to beloved mothers and fathers, aunts and uncles, children, successful businesses, treasured homes, irreplaceable family heirlooms, rich oral histories tracing back to Africa, and time-honored recipes, lost in the ashes of the Tulsa Race Massacre was Black economic *power*.

In the years after, Black business owners sifted through the soot and ashes to rebuild Greenwood on their own. Despite discriminatory lending and continued threats of violence, they made some strides, but any progress was stymied by gentrification. In the 1960s, four major highways were built; the one running through Tulsa cut off Black businesses. More rounds of urban renewal in the 1970s and 1980s further hampered the area's economic prospects. Today, most Black residents have been displaced and are found in North Tulsa where, according to Human Rights Watch, "some 33.5 percent of North Tulsans live in poverty, compared to 13.4 percent in South Tulsa. Unemployment overall for black people is 2.4 times the rate for white people. There are huge differences in life expectancy between north and south. North Tulsa has no traditional supermarkets with fresh meats and produce, and it is hard to find nutritious foods."[7] Instead of inheriting the significant wealth that could have been handed down among generations of Greenwood families, descendants inherited the suffocating systemic oppression that destroyed Black Wall Street more than one hundred years ago.

The Tulsa Race Massacre is among a long list of successful attempts to sabotage wealth and power building among Black, Indigenous, Latino, and Asian communities. Oklahoma in the 1920s was also the setting of the so-called Osage Reign of Terror, an epidemic of murders and mysterious deaths to steal oil-rich land from Osage Indians, who were the wealthiest people, per capita, on the planet.[8] Between 1910 and 1920, lynchings and executions of Mexican Americans in Texas counties along the US-Mexico border were motivated by a thirst for land owned by Tejanos.[9] The Rock Springs Massacre in 1885 was led by a white mob of coal miners who saw Chinese immigrant workers in the coal mines as a threat to their wages, leading them to kill twenty-eight Chinese people, injure fifteen others, and level the Chinatown neighborhood.[10]

The fear of communities of color amassing wealth has been and continues to be an implicit danger. To appease it, a powerful combination of savage violence and cunning legislation were deployed leading up to and throughout the twentieth century. From America's early beginnings, legislation was used to oppress and marginalize. In 1639, Virginia passed the first law to exclude "Negroes" from normal governmental protections. In 1936, in the midst of the Great Depression and high unemployment, Colorado banished all of the state's Mexicans and blockaded its southern border to keep them from returning.[11] Until 1978, Native American children could be legally taken from their families by the US government and sent to boarding schools to erase their Native culture, social ties, and traditions.[12] In 2023, despite the country's centuries-long practice of excluding people of color from quality education, the US Supreme Court struck down race-conscious college admissions that attempted to address these wrongs. The ruling opened a Pandora's box of legal challenges on the fairness of grants for Black female entrepreneurs and of diversity, equity, and inclusion (DEI) programs in schools, companies, and other organizations. Justice Ketanji Brown Jackson, the first Black woman to serve on the Supreme Court since it was established in 1789, said in her dissenting opinion: "Our country has never been colorblind. Given the lengthy history of state-sponsored race-based preferences in America, to say that anyone is now victimized if a college considers whether that legacy of discrimination has unequally advantaged its applicants fails to acknowledge the well-documented 'intergenerational transmission of inequality' that still plagues our citizenry."[13]

Today, undeniably brutal attacks still occur, but modern endeavors to keep money out of the hands of Black and Brown families are often more complex, ambiguous, and surreptitiously packaged in public policies, red tape, and rhetoric. Politicians don't have to name any racial or ethnic group in a proposed policy in order for it to hurt them. Republican campaign consultant Lee Atwater explained in a 1981 interview that the party could appeal to voters with racist views without having to use racist language. He was working as a strategist for President Ronald Reagan at the time.

> You start out in 1954 by saying, "Nigger, nigger, nigger." By 1968 you can't say "nigger"—that hurts you, backfires. So you say stuff like, uh, forced busing, states' rights, and all that stuff, and you're getting so abstract. Now, you're talking about cutting taxes, and all these things you're talking about are totally economic things and a byproduct of them is, blacks get hurt worse than whites. . . . "We want to cut this," is much more abstract than even the busing thing, uh, and a hell of a lot more abstract than "Nigger, nigger."

These tactics have proven effective. Today, white Americans hold ten times more total wealth than Black Americans and are twenty-eight times more likely to become millionaires.[14] The average white family has a net worth of $919,000 compared to $192,000 for Hispanic families.[15] Native Americans have the lowest educational achievement rates, with just 15 percent having a bachelor's degree or higher compared to 33.5 percent of whites.[16]

Race is at the uncomfortable center of poverty in America. It is the flicker, the tiny spark, the miniscule carbon particles that give way to vast disparities between the families that have and the families that don't have in this country. It has guided policymaking for centuries at every level of government, keeping prosperity and wealth out of the hands of Black and Brown communities, including the ability to pursue and complete higher education. It shapes our thoughts and opinions about deservedness and worth, potential and ability, and guilt and innocence. It lies beneath the surface of the struggle for justice in this country, the ugly underbelly of progress. For anyone who feels that we have moved beyond racism, the statistics above prove otherwise. In their book *Race in America*, Matthew Desmond and Mustafa Emirbayer tell us, "Racism persists as the cancer of American life."[17]

I didn't know my grandmother well. I knew her in the superficial way a granddaughter knows her grandmother, gleaned from birthday cards, phone calls, and rare visits. While I was in college in 2001, she died of heart disease, the number-one killer of Black women in America for numerous reasons, including unusually high levels of chronic stress.[18] The breathlessness, coughing, and wheezing consumed her before I could ask her the questions that I wish I could ask now, like what she envisioned for her life when she allowed herself to daydream and what stories were passed down in our family. Her nickname was Honey, and there was never a good explanation for that. Two of her sisters' nicknames were Boots and Babe, also for reasons I'll probably never know. She was the fifth of ten children born to Eleanyer Alberta Hannans and her husband, James Abraham Hannans, on April 16, 1912, in Georgia or Florida (the records are murky). Eleanyer, my great grandmother, gave birth to Honey at the same age I gave birth to my oldest daughter, Nerissa—nineteen. We were young Black mothers with eighty years between us, our lives immensely different and formidably similar at the same time.

In 1930, Honey graduated from the high school department of what was then Bethune-Cookman College in Daytona Beach, Florida—an extraordinary accomplishment at a time when very few Black children had the opportunity to attend, let alone complete, high school. In the 1930s, about 40 percent of the nation's Black workers were farm laborers, sharecroppers, and tenant farmers.[19] Sharecropping—a system where a landlord allows a tenant to work the land in exchange for a share of the crop—was a hard life. Children began picking cotton and tobacco and weeding rice plants in the fields as early as six years old. Only 14 percent of Black fifteen- to nineteen-year-olds were enrolled in public secondary schools in the South in 1932, partly because they needed to work the fields to help their families survive and partly because there were so few for Black students.[20] In 1933, across four states—Florida, Louisiana, Mississippi, and South Carolina—only sixteen Black high schools were accredited for four-year study, schools starved of funding, resources, and trained teachers.[21]

But Honey was fortunate enough to live near Bethune-Cookman. Educator and activist Mary McLeod Bethune, whose mother and grandmother were born enslaved, started the Daytona Literary and Industrial Training School for Negro Girls in 1904, with just $1.50 and five little girls in a rented house in a Black neighborhood. It later merged with the Cookman Institute for Boys in Jacksonville, Florida, founded in 1872 as the state's first institution of higher education for Black people. As the school grew, so did Bethune's vision for equality for Black girls and women, not only in education but in every facet of life. In 1920, she worked to register and mobilize Black voters in Daytona. As a result, the number of new Black voters soon surpassed that of new white voters in the city. In retaliation and fear, more than a hundred KKK members marched across the campus in white robes with signs that read "white supremacy" that year, and again just before the elections in 1922. After instructing the staff to take the students to their rooms for safety, Bethune stood immovable and resolute in the middle of the school buildings, as the Klan marched past. They didn't set fire to the school on either of those nights—though it wouldn't have been surprising if they had. The year before, just four states over, Greenwood had been set ablaze. But these buildings endured, and Honey joined hundreds of other students on campus years later.

Today, Bethune-Cookman University has a total undergraduate enrollment of 2,628,[22] the majority of whom are Black women.[23] Seventy-three percent of Bethune-Cookman students are awarded Pell Grants, federal grants for undergraduate students with exceptional financial need.[24] That's more than double the national average.[25] Bethune-Cookman is one of 101 historically Black colleges and universities (HBCUs) in the US,[26] schools established before 1964 to provide higher education to Black Americans denied access due to legal segregation and systemic oppression. For years, HBCUs provided the only pathway to economic mobility for Black families. In short, if you didn't go to an HBCU, you weren't going to college. The impact of these institutions is undeniable: they have educated 40 percent of today's Black engineers, 50 percent of today's Black lawyers, 70 percent of today's Black doctors, and 80 percent of Black judges in this country.[27] Without institutions like Bethune-Cookman, today's racial wealth gap between Black and White families would be even greater.

A little over one hundred years after enslaved people in the US were officially freed with the ratification of the Thirteenth Amendment to the Constitution, only 4.3 percent of students at non-HBCU institutions in the South were Black.[28] HBCUs were born out of need, out of an understanding that education is a vital pathway to wealth and prosperity, one that had been intentionally denied to Black Americans. From the institution of slavery that dehumanized Africans to the Jim Crow laws of the 1950s that legalized and fortified segregation to the recent Supreme Court rulings limiting race-based college admissions, barriers to higher education have persisted. To help families in poverty—families that are disproportionately Black and Brown—climb out of the constant state of struggle, this same understanding must be embraced. Quality education and educational opportunities have always been luxuries for families with few resources not by coincidence but by design. Telling a parent in poverty to "go back to school" or "get an education" as a solution without acknowledging the racist policies both past and present that have made it nearly impossible is like asking them to cross the ocean without a boat.

There are parents who *do* enroll in college, squeezing courses in between long shifts, draining commutes, homework, doctor's appointments, dinner prep, baths, and bedtime. They total about 22 percent of all college students.[29] Student parents are more likely than students without children to be people of color: 51 percent compared with 46 percent of students without children. According to a 2018 report by the Institute for Women's Policy Research and Ascend at the Aspen Institute, "Black college students are the most likely to be parents (33 percent), and Black women—two in five of whom are mothers—are more likely than women from other backgrounds to be raising children while in college." At my organization, 90 percent of our families are families of color.

Before one book club discussion, the event organizer pulled me aside to say that the group was struggling to understand a concept from my first book: the connection between racism and teen pregnancy. It was hard for some to grasp how racist policies and practices could lead to someone having a child at a young age—and how those same forces could contribute to single motherhood or having children before enrolling in college. As we sat in a circle, I asked them to imagine what it means to grow up in an environment starved of resources, starting from birth.

The exercise went something like this. As a Black or Brown child, you may come into the world having absorbed the consequences of poor prenatal care because pregnant women of color, particularly Black women, are more likely to be discriminated against by healthcare professionals.[30] Consequences like being born too early or having a low birth weight increase your risk for learning disabilities and developmental delays.[31] Arriving home from the hospital, you may experience unstable housing, from couch surfing to a pending eviction, as Native and Black Americans have higher rates of homelessness than other racial and ethnic groups.[32] Children without permanent housing have higher rates of illness, food insecurity (not having access to sufficient food or quality food), and emotional and behavioral problems.[33] As a toddler, you may not have a quality early childhood education that would help to position you for long-term academic success, as only 1 percent of Latino children and 4 percent of Black children are enrolled in high-quality state preschool programs.[34] Your K–12 education might be marked by outdated textbooks, substandard materials, lab equipment, and computers; overcrowded classes; underqualified teachers; fewer guidance counselors; and less access to rigorous curriculum, as the US educational system remains one of the most unequal among industrialized nations.[35]

You may have negative perceptions about school not just because of a subpar educational experience but also because as a Black or Latino student, you are more likely to be suspended than white students for the same infractions.[36] While research shows that high-quality after-school or extracurricular activities can enhance academic outcomes and social-emotional learning, as a Black child, you are less likely to participate in these opportunities because your family may not be able to afford them or access them in your school or neighborhood.[37] Woven together, these experiences could result in a series of disappointing report cards. Fourth-grade math scores on the National Assessment of Educational Progress (NAEP), also known as the Nation's Report Card, show 55 percent of Black fourth graders and 64 percent of Hispanic fourth graders achieve at least NAEP Basic or above, which indicates partial mastery, compared to 86 percent of white students. These percentages are similar for reading scores.[38] There is a connection between academics and teen pregnancy. Studies show that, among other factors, young people with lower grades have higher rates of teen pregnancy and birth.[39]

There aren't significant differences in sexual activity among Black and white teenagers,[40] but as a young person of color, you are more likely to have a baby young. The same healthcare system that may not have adequately cared for your mother may now discriminate against you, withholding information on effective birth control and contraceptives. If you're a Black teen girl who happens to become pregnant and lives in the South where more than half (56 percent) of the US Black population lives,[41] you may have limited access to an abortion because this is also an area of the country where states have banned the procedure. The 2022 US Supreme Court decision overturning *Roe v. Wade*, leaving the legality of abortion to the states, is disproportionately impacting people of color. They face structural barriers like limited access to healthcare, fewer financial resources, and an inability to travel out of state for abortion care.[42] And if you are a Native American teen girl, you are more likely to experience pregnancy and limited educational or career opportunities. American Indian/Alaska Native teenagers have the highest teen birth rate among all groups.[43]

These experiences just scratch the surface of the deep disparities that shape the lives of Black, Latino, and Indigenous youth—and the undeniable role that race plays in outcomes—graduating from high school or incarceration, becoming a neuroscientist or teen pregnancy, enjoying a fulfilling career or unemployment, being able to watch their children grow up or premature death. And these outcomes don't end in youth. They follow people into adulthood, often trapping parents in low-wage jobs that don't cover the costs of raising children. Far from exhaustive, the exercise helps illustrate how racism and oppression ultimately strip away choice, power, and autonomy in ways that profoundly impact what happens to us.

These connections weren't immediately visible to the book club members, connections that many struggle to see, overshadowed by the narrative that racism and its ripple effects are a thing of the past. In reality, something as powerful as the subjugation and oppression of whole nations of people cannot stand alone, bifurcated from what's happening in their lives, in their families, and in our country today. Chief Si'ahl, a leader of the Suquamish and Duwamish Native American tribes in what is now Washington state, put it this way: "Humankind has not woven the web of life. We are but one thread within it. Whatever we do to the web, we do to ourselves. All things are bound together. All things connect."[44]

Parents of color who want a postsecondary credential and the economic returns it can bring are up against exhausting logistics—caregiving, working full- or part-time, commuting to campus, and so on—as well as significant systemic disadvantages because of their racial and ethnic identity. More than 15 million undergraduate students were enrolled in degree-granting institutions in the fall of 2021. Of those students, 7.8 million were white, 3.3 million were Hispanic, 1.9 million were Black, 1.1 million were Asian, 663,100 were of two or more races, 107,000 were American Indian/Alaska Native, and 41,000 were Pacific Islander.[45] Those numbers show the racial and ethnic representation of students who enroll, but they don't speak to the other half of the equation: How many actually complete the degree?

Enrolling in college as a student of color is an achievement, and not simply because of the costs of higher education, which are particularly hard to shoulder. College affordability has become increasingly more challenging for all students, but American Indian/Alaska Native, Asian, Black, Hispanic/Latino, and Native Hawaiian/Pacific Islander students are more likely than white students to have unmet need. Almost nine in ten Black students face a gap between college costs and estimates of available resources.[46] Other obstacles—many identified in the exercise we just completed—add to making college unattainable. They include a dearth of Black and Brown K–12 teachers (80 percent of US teachers are white[47]); less access to college-ready courses in high school;[48] the impact of cultural insensitivity and bias from teachers, administrators, and classmates;[49] standardized college admission testing that favors wealthier students;[50] and other realities like increased police brutality against Black people[51] and the health effects of mining waste on Indian reservations.[52]

While other students are packing bathroom totes and twin comforters to embark on their college journeys, students of color carry with them injustices that plagued them in their K–12 experience. These include needing to work to afford college, to pay for housing, transportation, and food, and to help with family expenses; getting caught in a cycle of remedial classes that award no college credit but cost money; feeling excluded or isolated at predominantly white institutions; seeing the severe lack of Black and Latino faculty at most public four-year colleges and universities;[53] and being discriminated against in their academic programs.[54] The six-year graduation rates for first-time, full-time undergraduate students who started pursuing a bachelor's degree at a four-year institution in the fall of 2010 show the impacts of these barriers: Asian students (74 percent) have the highest completion rate, followed by white students (64 percent), students of two or more races (60 percent), Hispanic students (54 percent), Pacific Islander students (51 percent), Black students (40 percent), and American Indian/Alaska Native students (39 percent).[55] A 2023 report by the Lumina Foundation and Gallup found that nearly half of Black students in four-year programs considered stopping out of college in the past six months.[56]

All of this comes before factoring in the role of parenthood and its unique triumphs and challenges, especially in the context of race. For student parents, quality, affordable childcare is essential to earning a postsecondary credential. But if you're a Black parent, childcare is much harder to find, and it can consume more than half of your income.[57] With few colleges offering housing for undergraduates with children, most student parents have to live off campus and commute. As Jackie Powder notes in a *Hopkins Bloomberg Public Health* article, "For communities of color, unreliable mass transit, transportation costs, and unequal access have contributed to long-standing structural racism and associated socioeconomic barriers that have segregated communities from a range of opportunities." One of those opportunities is often higher education. Many students of color feel isolated on campus, but being a Black or Brown parenting student can make the experience even more isolating. A 2020 Generation Hope study found that 30 percent of parenting Black students and 25 percent of parenting Latino students felt either "somewhat unwelcome" or "very unwelcome" on their campuses compared to 16 percent of parenting white students.[58]

At Generation Hope, we often say that student-parent work—the effort to help more parents to and through college—is racial justice work. Success hinges upon our ability to dismantle long-standing oppressive policies and practices that have always worked against their ability to build wealth and power.

If these realities feel foreign to you, if race hasn't been a part of your understanding of families, poverty, and education in America, it's not because they aren't real. Nigerian author Chimamanda Ngozi Adichie writes in her novel *Americanah*, "Race doesn't really exist for you because it has never been a barrier."[59] If you've never felt the pain, suffering, or suffocation of a racist remark, action, or system, you've moved through the world with an extraordinary level of access. Perhaps you have felt the barrier of race but considered it a parallel cataclysm, separate from poverty, rather than the tangled together, inseparable roots shooting through the dark, damp piece of earth that is America. If this has been your understanding, as it was mine for years, I bring us back to Chief Si'ahl's words, "All things are bound together. All things connect."

After Honey finished high school at Bethune-Cookman, she didn't go on to earn a college degree or pursue a fulfilling career. Instead, she became a domestic worker, like the enslaved Black women before her, most Black women during her time, and nearly a third (28 percent) of Black women working in service jobs today.[60] She cooked, cleaned, and took care of other people's children while her own had to learn to make do alone. My father often told me she was famous for her chocolate cakes and sweet potato pies—treats he looked forward to when he came home from Tennessee State University, his HBCU alma mater. I often imagine her hands—the color of the pecans that fell from the tree in her backyard—moving around the perimeter of the pan, pinching the edges of the crust. And I wonder: *What was she passionate about?* If she had had a say in shaping her life, where might she have ended up? Had anyone ever asked her these things or was there an unspoken risk in dreaming that kept such questions buried? And after a lifetime of being told what to hope for and what she was *allowed* to be, would she even have the answers? At twenty-six, eight years after she finished high school, she gave birth to a daughter—my aunt—and became a single mother, with even less time to dream.

Maybe because of Honey, maybe because of how close my own experience as a young mother brought me to burying my own dreams, I can't help but look at people—all people—and wonder about theirs, about what they imagined for themselves if they had been free to pursue their passions without fear, without having to keep their heads down just to survive. I think about Greenwood—each of the residents and the entire community—and I wonder what *would have been* for those families and for the larger Black community in Oklahoma if the fire had never started, if the tiny spark never took hold, if the mob had never gathered, if Dick Rowland had never gotten into the elevator with that white woman, if the Klan's membership hadn't swelled, and if the neighboring white communities actually celebrated Black progress. The question is, of course, just a historical exercise, but it invites us to think about the present and the future, about what fires we need to ignite and what fires we must extinguish.

CHAPTER 3

GENDER AND OUR COMPANIONS

Telling our story is an invitation. In our vulnerability, the audience finds a companion on their own journey of reflection through their glittering celebrations and wins to their somber, solitary moments. I never anticipated becoming a safe place for others to ruminate on the twists and turns of their own lives when I sat down to write about my triumphs and defeats as a young mother, but this intimate dialogue as both strangers and old friends is now one of my favorite things about writing. Sometimes I have the opportunity to meet my traveling companions in real life, and our brief exchanges often come with instant understanding, familiarity, and connection because—together—we have been through something.

Once after I spoke at a conference, an older white woman with large, sophisticated Coco Chanel–style eyeglasses and long, silky white hair twisted into an elegant bun, waited in line to say hello. She held a copy of my book tightly against her canary yellow dress, and when it was her turn, she stepped forward, extended a thin, soft hand and gently gripped my wrist. Her glassy eyes prompted me to lay my hand over hers, and she proceeded to tell me she was moved by my book because it made her think about the baby she carried as a sixteen-year-old, a baby no one knew about, including her husband and children, because she never brought it into the world. Afraid of what her life would become and how she would support a child as a young, single mother in a world that judged so harshly and withheld support, she told me, through tears, that all those years ago, she had an abortion. Reading my book was the first time, in a long time, that she allowed herself to think about her sixteen-year-old self, the baby, her decision, and the world that takes away our choices. I asked if I could hug her, and we stood together for several minutes, connected by our stories of love, grief, strength, and forgiveness.

What is the cost of shame? There are quantifiable, monetary losses. Jobs we don't take, contests we don't enter, businesses we don't start. And then there are intangible losses. Things that can't be measured easily, like never finding or using our voice, meeting people who could change our lives, believing we deserve a healthy relationship rather than a dangerous one. Unlike guilt, which is a bad feeling about something we've done or said, author, professor, and researcher Brené Brown defines shame as "the intensely painful feeling or experience of believing that *we* are flawed and therefore unworthy of love and belonging."[1] There are costs, sometimes terrible costs, to believing we are innately bad.

When Generation Hope partners with colleges across the country to help them build more family-inclusive campuses, our focus on shame often surprises them. At first, it may seem unrelated to important topics like collecting data on the parenting status of their students (something most colleges don't do) or adding more lactation spaces (required under the Affordable Care Act for employees but often lacking for students). But shame is, in fact, central to the work of helping parents earn degrees and families transcend poverty.

I was introduced to the power of shame as a brown-skinned child growing up in a predominantly white New England town, made to believe that something was wrong with me because I wasn't white. And I was still unprepared for how becoming a teen mother would challenge the way I thought about myself. I had to resist believing I was inherently bad when I lost most of my high school friends after my pregnancy and when other parents at my daughter's childcare center wouldn't sit with me during meetings. I carried these experiences into the design of our programming at Generation Hope. We had to challenge the notion that our students were innately flawed, an unrelenting message that likely burdened them long before their pregnancies. If you are Black or Brown, you hear and see this message on television shows and the local news from an early age. If you are a woman, you internalize this message as soon as you are old enough to play with Barbie dolls. If you grow up in public housing or don't have new clothes on the first day of school, your classmates taunt you with this message on the bus. In getting to know our Scholars, the student parents we bring on as fellows in our institutional work, and parents across the country, the theme of shame surfaces over and over. Sometimes they don't have a name or label for it—instead they use words like *unworthy*, *bad*, or *failing*—but each of them, in different ways, shares how shame has shaped them. And while we hear it occasionally from fathers, most often, it is mothers who express this internalized story.

Brené Brown was motivated to begin formally researching shame after becoming a mother. She explains: "Women often experience shame when they are entangled in a web of layered, conflicting and competing social-community expectations. Shame leaves women feeling trapped, powerless and isolated."[2] These expectations are almost always impossible to meet, and "present very narrow interpretations of who women are 'supposed to be' based on demographics (i.e., their gender, race, class, sexual orientation, age, religious identity) and/or our roles (i.e., a mother, an employee, a partner, a group member)." Expectations are powerful. From a very young age, girls are conditioned to follow the rules, to be kind, soft, supportive, nurturing, clean, pretty, and not too ambitious. It is who they are "supposed to be." To be otherwise, to deviate from these norms, is to be *bad*. A tool of oppression, the fear of embodying failure robs women of their choices and their freedom. Once we believe something is wrong with us, shame seeps into every facet of our lives. The elegant woman I met that day after my keynote understood these expectations and fears as a teenage girl, and by the time we met many years later, I imagine she understood them even more deeply as an older woman who had lived so much of her life.

While these expectations plague all women, they are unrelenting for women in poverty, especially mothers. Their day-to-day survival doesn't fit the image of "good" and "right," making shame harder to deflect.

Working long hours away from their children and often on their feet, advocating for their family at the social services office over and over again, not being able to make every parent-teacher conference or school play, struggling to pay rent—never mind keeping the house clean—antagonize feelings of belonging, worthiness, and connection. In subtle and overt ways, society tells women in poverty that they are failing while simultaneously making it harder for them to succeed. And if they desire more, if they want to further their education by finishing high school or going to college, they are shamed for too much ambition, selfishly focusing on themselves rather than just working to provide for their families.

In America, women are 35 percent more likely than men to live in poverty.[3] Women of color have the highest rates of poverty. About one in four American Indian/Alaska Native women experience poverty, the highest among women or men of any racial or ethnic group.[4] For anyone who assumes that women are more likely to live in poverty because they aren't working, it's important to note that women also make up a larger share of the working poor. According to the National Women's Law Center, "Across the United States, more than 22.2 million people work in the forty lowest paying jobs—and women make up nearly two-thirds (64 percent) of this workforce."[5] More than a quarter of women in the low-paid workforce have at least one child under eighteen at home, and the vast majority of these mothers, especially Black mothers, are the sole or primary breadwinners for their families.[6] Overall, single mothers have higher rates of poverty with nearly a quarter of unmarried mothers living below the poverty line.[7] In short, poverty and shame are disproportionately shouldered by single mothers in this country.

When Venus Williams walked into the boardroom at the All England Lawn Tennis and Croquet Club in 2005 the day before the Wimbledon women's final, no one knew exactly what she'd say to the members of the Grand Slam Committee, executives from the four Grand Slam tournaments—the Australian Open, Roland-Garros, Wimbledon, and the US Open. She was expected to touch upon the parity in prize money to the men's and women's champions but how far she would push was unclear. Williams, twenty-five, a decorated athlete and celebrity, and one of only two women in attendance, began by asking everyone to close their eyes and then said:

> Imagine you're a little girl. You're growing up. You practice as hard as you can, with girls, with boys. You have a dream. You fight, you work, you sacrifice to get to this stage. You work as hard as anyone you know. And then you get to this stage, and you're told you're not the same as a boy. Almost as good, but not quite the same. Think how devastating and demoralizing that could be.

She was voicing her frustrations and a call-to-action in the enduring fight for equal pay for women in the US—one of the chronic sources of women's economic need. Simply put, women are paid less than men for doing the same job or providing the same service. In 2021, women earned about eighty-two cents for every dollar men earned. Compared to white men, Hispanic or Latina women earned about fifty-eight cents for every dollar earned, and Black women earned about sixty-three cents.[8] Unequal pay makes it difficult to meet immediate needs like filling a gas tank or paying for a prescription. It also prevents women from saving over time and building wealth at the same rate as men. There is no nest egg to cover emergencies like a failing car transmission or a broken window in your home. Their children's needs, from a new school uniform to braces, also become insurmountable. When women want to make investments in themselves or their families, such as paying for courses at their local community college to become a social worker or putting a down payment on a home, they lack the resources. And discriminatory practices keep those resources even further from their reach. According to the Center for American Progress, "Women are more likely to be denied mortgages and to be overcharged for them; are particularly vulnerable to predatory lending; hold more debt; and face other obstacles that undermine their ability to build wealth and savings."[9]

Women disproportionately experience poverty because they earn less than men for the same jobs. They are also more likely to be working in low-paying occupations. Jobs as childcare professionals, bartenders, fast-food workers, hotel clerks, housekeeping staff, and home health aides come with smaller paychecks and few to no protections. More than one in six employed women in the United States work in low-paid jobs.[10] Those jobs often come with inflexible and unpredictable schedules, making it difficult to parent or continue their education. Without employer-sponsored benefits, such as retirement plans, health insurance, paid sick and maternity leave, and paid vacations, it becomes nearly impossible to plan for the future, access medical care for themselves or their children, take time off to care for a new child, or have a much-needed break from work. More than 60 percent of low-wage workers, most of whom are women, don't have access to paid sick days.[11] For these women, keeping their family afloat is a herculean task, not just because they have less money in their pockets but because they have to stay employed without being able to recover from giving birth, afford a doctor's visit, or stay home with a child who is running a fever. Nineteen percent of women working in low-wage jobs report losing employment because they were sick or caring for a sick child,[12] and 80 percent worry that they won't be able to balance work with the needs of their families.[13]

Large global summits and national conferences are held each year to identify the most effective ways to dismantle poverty with some of the most educated people in the world presenting complex strategies, but the real solutions are actually uncomplicated and quite clear—especially to those who are most impacted. Madeleine M. Kunin, the first woman to serve as governor of Vermont, put it simply: "The best antidote to poverty remains simple—a paycheck. Policies like paid family leave, workplace flexibility and affordable quality childcare can make the difference for two-parent or single-parent working families who struggle to make ends meet."[14] Janelle Jones, the first Black woman to serve as chief economist at the US Department of Labor, provides an even more specific solution. She introduced the "Black Women Best" philosophy, a foundational economic principle that argues that when we center Black women's economic well-being in our policymaking, everyone thrives. If you design solutions that make it easier for Black women, who disproportionately bear the burden of economic hardship in the US and have been most harmed by its systems, then suffering will be alleviated for everyone.

Najah, a Black mother of four, graduated from the University of Maryland in 2024. But before she walked proudly across the stage in her black cap and gown, she navigated years of housing and food insecurity while trying to care for her family. In 2023, as a part of our advocacy work, we asked her to write an op-ed that appeared in *The Grio* about an unseen but arduous foe in her pursuit of a postsecondary credential and a better life for her children—public benefits. She wrote:

> Programs like cash assistance, food stamps and other public benefits are supposed to be a resource for parents, especially mothers, to provide for their families. However, legislative changes and inflexible requirements over the years have made it more difficult for parents to not only utilize these programs but to navigate beyond them.[15]

Najah's challenging experience is the norm rather than the exception. Like Najah, I've waited in long lines to get food stamps with a baby on my hip while I was supposed to be in class. I've heard exhaustion in the voices of families across the country who haven't been able to navigate the red tape and bureaucracy that guard these resources. Often the design and rollout of public benefit programs help *keep* people in poverty rather than traverse it.

As Najah described, public benefit programs generally don't meet the needs of families and aren't widely accessible. The Supplemental Nutrition Assistance Program (SNAP) feeds roughly forty million people. But eligibility rules and enrollment processes are complicated and confusing, benefits don't reflect what households require for an adequate diet, and families often struggle after SNAP benefits run out (often just two weeks after receipt). Unemployment insurance, a joint state-federal program, provides cash benefits to eligible workers, but the level of support varies from state to state, and women are often deemed ineligible because they are more likely to work part-time and to resign from jobs to take care of children. The Special Supplemental Nutrition Program for Women, Infants, and Children (WIC) provides food, information on health and nutrition, education, and support to 1.5 million low-income women and children up to age five. But only half of eligible pregnant women receive WIC benefits nationally.[16] Temporary Assistance for Needy Families (TANF), the federal program that provides grants to states to support families' basic needs, has rigid work requirements that disincentivize parents from attending college, funding that has lagged behind inflation, and complex, burdensome eligibility requirements. At its peak in 1994, TANF reached 5.1 million families. That number had declined to 1 million by 2022.[17] And these safety net programs—which aren't even reaching all of the families across the country that are struggling to afford food and housing, many of which are headed by women—are under attack by legislators who believe they are unnecessary or ineffective.

Unworthy and *undeserving* aren't words that we usually associate with how laws are made in this country. While women have powered the US economy, often to the detriment of their own well-being and that of their families, certain groups of women have been forced—through discriminatory policies—to sacrifice even more based on these words and the beliefs behind them. Aid to Dependent Children (ADC), an early welfare program that began as a part of the Social Security Act of 1935 during the Great Depression, was designed to help widowed white women stay home to care for their children. Until the 1960s, caseworkers didn't distribute this cash assistance to most poor Black mothers because the expectation was that they work rather than stay at home like white mothers. This forced Black women to take low-wage jobs to provide for their children, often working for white families. In his book *American Dream: Three Women, Ten Kids, and a Nation's Drive to End Welfare*, Jason DeParle notes that pressures to end racial discrimination under ADC contributed to a shift, and by 1960, 40 percent of the recipients were Black. There were also more single and divorced mothers receiving cash benefits rather than widows. Black. Single. Divorced. Unworthy. Undeserving. Anti-welfare backlash was imminent.

TANF, the cash benefit program that Najah describes and that I tried to navigate as a young mother in college, was born out of the 1996 welfare reform law, officially called the Personal Responsibility and Work Opportunity Act, signed by President Bill Clinton. While the law promised to drastically decrease the need for welfare, years later, it was clear that it had instead significantly increased extreme poverty and left families without a safety net[18]—and they were disproportionately families of color.[19] Although it was President Clinton who signed the legislation, the groundwork had been laid years before, building upon a legacy of racist beliefs dating back to slavery. Those beliefs cast women of color, particularly Black women, as unfit mothers, better suited for labor than caring for their children, and capable of only certain types of jobs. In the early 1970s, President Richard Nixon's diligent work on welfare reform was colored by his own beliefs. Former Nixon Presidential Library director Tim Naftali described those beliefs plainly:

> The 37th president of the United States was a racist: He believed in treating people according to their race, and that race implied fundamental differences in individual human beings. Nixon's racism matters to us because he allowed his views on race to shape U.S. policies—both foreign and domestic. His policies need to be viewed through that lens.[20]

In the 1980s, President Ronald Reagan campaigned against Aid to Families with Dependent Children (renamed in 1962 to be more inclusive of the whole family) by frequently invoking the welfare queen stereotype: a Black single mother exploiting the system by having more children to increase her cash benefits. The trope successfully fueled the anti-welfare, pro-work requirement movement and accelerated support for President Clinton's welfare reform years later. Johnnie Tillmon, a divorced Black mother of six from President Clinton's home state of Arkansas, an activist on the front lines of the welfare debate during the 1960s and '70s, described how these efforts stripped Black women of their dignity and value: "I'm a Black woman. I'm a poor woman. I'm a fat woman. I'm a middle-aged woman. And I'm on welfare. In this country, if you're any one of those things you count less as a human being. If you're all those things, you don't count at all."[21]

Like Johnnie and Honey, women of color have been treated as *less than*, not meeting the standard of "good" and "right," and subsequently segregated into low-wage jobs for centuries. Black women have always worked in poorly paid agriculture jobs—on farms sowing seeds, weeding, harvesting, and selling produce—and domestic service occupations—cooking, cleaning, and taking care of children.[22] By 1900, 95 percent of all Black women in the US spent long days in the hot sun tending to crops or on their feet working in someone else's home.[23] Even after the Great Migration, one of the largest internal movements in US history when approximately six million Black people relocated from the South to Northern, Midwestern, and Western states between the 1910s and

1970s, most employers continued to limit Black women to domestic work.[24] They migrated to escape racial violence and pursue economic and educational opportunities that were impossible under Jim Crow only to find their freedom similarly stifled in these new places. The continuation and ripple effects of this discrimination have endured. Today, nearly a third (28 percent) of Black women are employed in service jobs compared to one-fifth of white women,[25] and 50 percent of working women of color make less than fifteen dollars an hour compared to 26 percent of white workers.[26] In 2023, after introducing the Raise the Wage Act to increase the federal minimum wage to seventeen dollars by 2028, benefiting nearly twenty-eight million workers, Senator Bernie Sanders of Vermont said, "A job should lift you out of poverty, not keep you in it."[27] For millions of women, particularly women of color and single mothers, their jobs are a daily struggle rather than a pathway toward opportunity and advancement.

Most Americans believe that hard work and grit influence whether or not someone will be successful in this country. Education ranks fifth in importance, and gender and race are second to last on the list.[28] No matter how hard or how many hours a woman works, her inability to provide for her family is more likely to be attributed to her laziness, lack of ambition, and poor choices rather than external and societal factors that keep success out of her reach. Dragging these anchors of gender and racial discrimination into a college classroom requires terrific determination and fortitude, yet 70 percent of all parenting college students are mothers who somehow find a way to make it to campus. The majority of those mothers are single and often shoulder all, or a good portion, of their family's financial needs and have even less time between working and parenting to devote to their studies. After pushing through the shaming and stigmatization that would tempt even the strongest-willed person to give up, they enroll in college only to find similar hurdles within higher education. Only 8 percent of single mothers who start college earn an associate's or bachelor's degree within six years, not just for reasons outside of the classroom but for a myriad of reasons within it.[29]

During one book club discussion over Zoom, a woman unmuted herself and shared that years earlier she had attempted college, but on the first day of class, after introducing herself during the round-robin and talking about giving birth to her daughter just two weeks earlier, the professor asked with a confused look: "Why are you here?" She ran out of the room in tears and didn't come back to any of her classes. In her forties, she enrolled at an institution that embraced her role as a parent, and she went on to earn a bachelor's degree and then a master's degree. I haven't been able to shake that story and the power of those four words: "Why are you here?" Mothers in college are asked this question literally and figuratively every day. If it's not asked by a professor, a fellow student, or an administrator behind a desk, it is communicated in other ways. Like when a financial aid officer fails to share resources for covering the costs of childcare, information that could prevent a mom from having to stop out of school. Or a mom can't access lactation spaces to pump between classes so she is able to bring milk home to her baby. Or when inflexible attendance policies force a mom to come to class just days after having a C-section. Or when the only class that fits with a mom's work and childcare schedule fills up before her designated registration slot. Time and time again, mothers pursuing their education are asked: "Why are you here?"

More representation in leadership roles within colleges and universities could spark change, but systemic bias has kept too many women from the president's office, especially at major public and private schools. A 2022 reports *The Women's Power Gap at Elite Universities: Scaling the Ivory Tower*, released by the Eos Foundation's Women's Power Gap Initiative in partnership with the American Association of University Women, found that out of 130 high-level research (R1) schools, only 22 percent had a woman who was president, chancellor, or system head—and 46 percent had never had a woman in these roles. The problem isn't a lack of qualified candidates or an insufficient candidate pool. In fact, women have been earning the majority of PhDs in the US for roughly a decade.[30] The problem is a gender bias. The same gender bias that keeps mothers out of college and in low-wage jobs also keeps women out of influential positions of power within higher education.

More than fifty years ago, Edith Green, a member of Congress, helped to create Title IX, a federal law that prohibits discrimination against women in education. Green and her colleagues were motivated by years of educational inequality. It took more than two hundred years after the founding of Harvard, America's first institution of higher education, before women were admitted to college. The first woman enrolled at Oberlin College in 1837. Nearly thirty years after that, the first Black woman earned a bachelor's degree there. Since the beginning of higher education in this country, men were the target population for colleges and universities, not women and certainly not mothers. These exclusions continued, preventing women from attending certain schools, dissuading them from applying to various academic and athletic programs, and subjecting them to more scrutiny in the admissions process. Today, every college that receives federal funding is required to have a Title IX officer, and while often associated with protections against sexual assault and harassment on college campuses, Title IX also protects the rights of pregnant students and, with limited guidance, parenting students.

Title IX is just a starting point for ensuring that women and parents have equal access to higher education. More work is needed, including clearer, more visible language on college websites; comprehensive training for faculty, administrators, and staff on the rights and protections of pregnant and parenting students; greater awareness of the law among students themselves; and more explicit guidance on those protections after a child is born or enters a student's care. Title IX had been a law for twenty-seven years when I was raising my daughter at William & Mary, but I had no idea what it was or what rights I was entitled to. More than twenty years later, that remains the case for many parents trying to earn a degree. In a 2020 study, Generation Hope found that 51 percent of parenting students didn't know who to talk to about discrimination due to their parenting status.[31]

Representative Green understood why the passing of Title IX was just the beginning of the fight: "Let us not deceive ourselves. Our educational institutions have proven to be no bastions of democracy."[32]

Josh found out about being accepted into Generation Hope's Scholar Program not long before his mother went into hospice and passed away of stage four colon cancer. When he lost her, he lost his number-one supporter. Together, they had navigated his father abandoning the family when Josh was a teenager. He came home from school one day to find two large moving trucks parked outside. Together, they had helped

Josh's three younger sisters stay on track. Together, they had experienced the joys and challenges of Josh becoming a father at sixteen. Now he would have to figure out college—and so much more—without her. This wouldn't be easy, not as a father of three sons, with bills to pay and a history of negative experiences with the education system, including time in a juvenile detention center and leaving high school before eventually earning his GED. Young fathers like Josh often exist in the blurred background of efforts focused on family economic mobility, with only a slight recognition of their place in the equation.

Teen fathers, Black fathers, fathers of color, fathers experiencing poverty, they have all been lumped into the category of absent dads. In 1965, *The Negro Family: The Case for National Action*, or the Moynihan Report after its author, Assistant Secretary of Labor Daniel Patrick Moynihan, gave birth to the idea that the coming "crumbling" of Black families was caused by increasing rates of out-of-wedlock births and single-mother homes. In short, the absent father rather than systemic racism was to blame for the issues facing Black Americans. It is true that out-of-wedlock births have increased among all races since 1965; today, about 70 percent of Black children are born to parents who are not married.[33] But as former journalist Josh Levs points out in his book *All In: How Our Work-First Culture Fails Dads, Families, and Businesses—And How We Can Fix It Together*, most Black fathers live with their children, and a 2013 Centers for Disease Control and Prevention (CDC) report found that Black fathers are more involved with their children, whether they live with them or not, than fathers of other races.[34] But like many racist stereotypes, the myth persists, with consequences.

This erasure of fathers leads to little support for their educational aspirations, especially for Black, Latino, and Indigenous fathers, who already face systemic hurdles to enrolling in and staying in college. The gender gap in higher education has been on the rise since 1979. Currently three women are enrolled in college for every two men.[35] Women are also more likely to graduate from college than men. Research shows this graduation gender gap exists even in high school.[36] The numbers become bleaker when seen through the lens of race and ethnicity. Men of color have some of the lowest college graduation rates. Black men (38.6 percent) and Native American men (38.2 percent) have the lowest six-year completion rates for bachelor's degrees.[37] Of the more than two million bachelor's degrees earned during the 2019–20 academic year, only 12.9 percent went to men of color.[38] Experts list being first-generation college students, having to work full-time to help support their families, and not being able to afford college as reasons men of color aren't completing college at higher rates. While all of this is true, so are the subtle and not-so-subtle ways men of color are discouraged from academic achievement, discriminated against in school settings, deprived of role models who look like them in educational spaces, and funneled to prison rather than postsecondary success. In his article "Race and the Schooling of Black Americans," social psychologist and Stanford University professor Claude M. Steele reminds us of where America does prioritize Black men: "At any given time, nearly as many Black males are incarcerated as are in college in this country."

For all of these reasons, fathers, especially fathers of color, are among the most unlikely to stay in college and to one day hold a degree in their hands. Of all fathers who enroll at public four-year institutions, 70 percent stop out. For fathers who are raising children on their own, 71 percent stop out. When looking specifically at fathers of color, 72 percent of Black fathers and 66 percent of Latino fathers stop out. These student groups experience higher stop-out rates than student parents overall and student mothers, yet we rarely mention them in discussions on college completion, family economic mobility, and poverty.[39] It's as if they simply don't exist.

Josh ended up graduating with an associate of science degree in computer science and an associate of science degree in mathematics from Northern Virginia Community College in 2021, and then, in the fall of 2022, transferred to George Mason University's School of Engineering. Josh's Generation Hope mentor encouraged him to apply for the US Department of Defense's SMART Scholarship-for-Service Program, which offers full-tuition scholarships, internships, and guaranteed civilian employment with the Department of Defense after graduation for undergraduate, master's, and doctoral students pursuing a STEM degree. Josh was accepted into the program, providing both financial relief and career opportunities. In 2025, he graduated from ODUGlobal at Old Dominion University with a bachelor's degree in computer science. Still,

Josh will be the first to tell you that, even with his wife's unwavering support, his journey was incredibly hard. "I took exams in the delivery room. I had a physics quiz, computer science test, and calculus exam. Some professors encouraged me to take a W and withdraw, but I did schoolwork the whole time my wife was in the hospital." At any given time, the obstacles could have felt too big—the judgment too intense, the scrutiny too overwhelming, the sense of not belonging too powerful. And despite how smart he is, he might never have made it to the graduation stage like the majority of fathers who try but don't finish.

We will never truly see the mountains that families in poverty must climb without acknowledging that gender plays a role in their ascent—for both mothers and fathers. Despite our reluctance to talk about it, gender is always with us, casting a shadow on even large-scale attempts to accelerate economic mobility in this country. And it has always been with us. From the beginning, America was shaped by gendered policies—from stripping Native American women of the respect, authority, and decision-making they held before British colonizers arrived to incentivizing the rape of Black enslaved women by making their children the property of their masters.

In 1776, the year that America was born, women could not own property, control their own money, vote, or sign legal documents. One hundred and forty-four years later, women finally won the right to vote through the Nineteenth Amendment. One hundred and ninety-six years later, Title IX banned discrimination on the basis of sex in any program that receives financial assistance from the federal government. A year later, in 1973, the US Supreme Court ruled in *Roe v. Wade* that criminalizing abortion was unconstitutional, a decision that stood for almost fifty years before being overturned in 2022. Two hundred and eighteen years after the signing of the Declaration of Independence, the Violence Against Women Act allocated funds to address violent crimes against women, including rape, stalking, and domestic violence. And while the founding fathers wrote these famous words as the basis of our governmental system: "We hold these truths to be self-evident, that all men are created equal, that they are endowed by their Creator with certain unalienable Rights, that among these are Life, Liberty and the pursuit of Happiness," it would take another 244 years for a woman to serve as second-in-command. A woman has never served as president of the United States.

For these reasons and more, the fight is starkly different for mothers in poverty than it is for fathers in poverty, and then in some ways, it is heartbreakingly similar. What is undeniable is that our policies and systems restrict power, agency, and freedom on the basis of gender, muzzling potential and holding back generations of promise for millions of families, our country, and our world. Somewhere in the complex sea of biased legislation, harmful rhetoric, and oppressive practices are these very simple truths: a mother's success is our collective success, and a father's win is a win for all of us. As American actor and UN Women Goodwill Ambassador Anne Hathaway put it at the United Nations official commemoration of International Women's Day on March 8, 2017, in New York: "The whole world grows when people like you and me take a stand because we know that beyond the idea of how women and men are different, there is a deeper truth that love is love, and parents are parents."[40]

In January 2024, a news report from Hawaii shared a devastating story: a homeless woman, having just given birth on a sidewalk, was seen dragging her newborn baby by the umbilical cord down the street. Emergency crews were immediately called to the scene, and the baby, thankfully, was taken immediately to the hospital where it was said to be breathing and in stable condition. The image of this woman in the early Tuesday evening light, raw from birth, pulling a precious newborn baby girl behind her, haunts me. It reminds me of the women I've met who chose to end their pregnancies because of other people's expectations, like the one I hugged tightly after my keynote. It also reminds me of the women I've met who were forced to give birth to children they didn't want, the pressures of family, partners, or policies robbing them of their choice. It returns me to my question about the costs of shame and all that we lose—collectively—when we make someone believe that they are inherently *less than*. And as I think of this woman, I wonder how lonely, broken, and disconnected she must have been, not just that night, but in all the days that preceded it. How dark the world must have felt. How numb she must have become.

One of the first things I tell students new to our program is that they don't have to be perfect here. They don't have to hide a poor grade or a pending eviction or a suicidal thought. We want to know about the grade so we can connect them with a tutor, the pending eviction so we can provide emergency funding to keep them in their home, and the suicidal thought so we can get them the mental health support they need. I tell them this because I longed to hear it when I was a young mother experiencing challenge after challenge, even as I was making the dean's list at a prestigious college. I needed to hear that I wasn't experiencing those obstacles because something was wrong with me, something that I needed to keep hidden to survive. I needed to hear that these things were expected, not because I wasn't working hard enough or didn't have enough grit or because I was innately bad or unworthy or undeserving. No, these things were expected because something was wrong with the systems I was trying to navigate, and for that reason, what I was trying to do was hard. It was just hard. And it still is.

Instead of forcing our students to hide themselves and the challenges they face, we extend our hand and ask permission to join them on an inevitably difficult journey. They are apprehensive at first. For a lifetime they have been in lockstep with disparaging whispers that chip away at their self-worth. But soon, we show up, together, as ourselves, all of us imperfect and struggling, and their grip on our hand becomes a bit tighter. A friend's wise grandmother used to say we need people in our lives "who sing the song of our hearts back to us, to remind us of who we are." I like to think that that's one of the most important, unspoken parts of Generation Hope's work—we remind mothers and fathers of who they are on the days when it's most difficult to remember. We sing their heart song, a melody about how profoundly powerful and worthy they are. I've seen in my own life—and the lives of the parents we've had the honor to serve—that we are born anew when we aren't forced to contort ourselves into someone else's definition of "good" and "right." We make our own choices. We feel unbridled joy and frustration and connection. Instead of apologizing for our dreams, we chase them.

CHAPTER 4

MONEY AND BLOOD

The sounds of violence are distinct, haunting intonations. Piercing screams. Tumbling scuffles. Harrowing moans. Sometimes chilling silences. They startle us to attention, demanding a response. Even without having all of the details and testimonies, the sounds of an assault compel us to act, to do things we didn't know we had the courage to do, like holding a cloth against a gushing wound, calling the police, or directing an onlooker to run for help. Our fear of uninhibited violence creates in us an urgency, an unexpected bravery, and a nearly universal response that it must be stopped, *immediately*.

Violence feels easy to recognize, so obvious that a formal definition is unnecessary, yet the actual explanation for it is surprisingly vague: "an intense, turbulent, or furious and often destructive action or force."[1] This broader framing widens our view of violence beyond physical acts. We struggle with this larger lens, seeing harm only in its most simplistic and obvious forms—acts that bruise the body, pierce organs and tissue, strangle out breath, and lacerate the skin—but if we're honest, humans have a long, grisly history of exerting much more intricate and complex ways to inflict pain and destruction.

Loss and survival are teachers in the depths and many iterations of violence with lessons that either break us or strengthen our resolve to fight back. So many of us carry these lessons throughout our lives, but I imagine someone like Coretta Scott King had a particularly sophisticated understanding of violence. Each day, she sent her husband out into the world with the threat of murder or serious injury looming over their family. On a Thursday evening on April 4, 1968, in Memphis, Tennessee, those threats culminated in a fatal bullet wound to the lower right side of his face. Martin Luther King Jr. had been standing on a balcony outside his second-floor room at the Lorraine Motel, getting ready for dinner. The official autopsy, performed by Shelby County medical examiner Dr. Jerry T. Francisco, concluded that King's death was the result of a single "gunshot wound to the chin and neck with a total transaction of the lower cervical and upper thoracic spinal cord and other structures of the neck."[2] Dr. King was just thirty-nine years old.

In the devastation, Coretta Scott King was left to not only raise their four children, ranging from five to twelve years old, but to also carry on their shared work of creating a more just and loving world. On Mother's Day, just one month after burying her husband, raw with grief and loss, she courageously stood at the microphone at a rally in front of thousands of people, including members of the original Poor People's Campaign. From that podium she echoed the most common and pervasive violence that America has allowed to proliferate:

> I must remind you that starving a child is violence. Neglecting school children is violence. Punishing a mother and her family is violence. Discrimination against a working man is violence. Ghetto housing is violence. Ignoring medical need is violence. Contempt for poverty is violence.[3]

Instead of guns, knives, or bloodshed, she described starvation, neglect, punishment, discrimination, ignorance, and contempt as deadly weapons used to harm people. Even in the wake of her husband's murder, Coretta could see then what few people can now: the full spectrum of harm imposed upon people living in poverty every day. As her husband had done, she called for an end to systems of *economic violence* against the most underserved in this country. This battle cry and America's tolerance of the worst injustices were heavy on Dr. King's heart during his last days. In his third book, *Why We Can't Wait*, published just ten months before his assassination, he wrote, "Many white Americans of good will have never connected bigotry with economic exploitation. They have deplored prejudice, but tolerated or ignored economic injustice. But the Negro knows that these two evils have a malignant kinship."

Mississippi—a place Dr. King once said might determine the future of the United States because it was where "democracy faced its most serious challenge"—has the highest recorded number of lynchings in the country between 1882 and 1968: 581. These lynchings were more than just public killings. White mobs often tortured their victims with mutilation and beatings, decapitating them and desecrating their bodies. Some were even burned alive. Today, Mississippi is the state with the highest overall poverty rate (19.6 percent), the highest child poverty rate (27.9 percent), and the highest hunger and food insecurity rate (15.7 percent).[4] Black, Latino, and Native American residents are its most impoverished groups.[5] Destitution exists across the state, but it's most heavily concentrated along the Mississippi River, areas with the largest Black populations. The most common job for Black Mississippians, a cashier, is also one of the state's lowest-paying jobs, with a median earning of just $8.79 an hour.[6] Lynchings were just one of many ways to terrorize Black people. Keeping them in poverty was another. The Kings understood that physical violence and economic exploitation were tightly fastened together as tools of oppression against millions of Americans. One is harder to look away from. The other we have long tolerated, ignored, even condoned.

Economic violence is evident on street corners, where houseless people wrap in blankets to keep warm on freezing winter nights and in news stories about mothers jailed for trying to enroll their children in better school districts. But we feel little urgency to remedy or to stop it. These assaults—even those inflicted on children—have been normalized, dismissed as inevitable outcomes or blamed on laziness and apathy. We watch them unravel without feeling a call to action, an obligation to step in, or the bravery or courage to *do something*. We rarely stop to question the societal forces that make these gaping wounds so pervasive.

Poverty is deadly. It is the fourth-highest cause of deaths in America, behind heart disease, cancer, and smoking.[7] Living just one year in poverty is associated with 183,000 deaths in the US annually, and living in "cumulative poverty"—defined as ten years or more—is associated with 295,000 deaths per year.[8] That's more than the number of people who die each year from drug overdose, suicide, and firearms combined. According to the US Department of Agriculture, one in five children in this country don't know where they will get their next meal. Food insecurity causes changes to how their brains develop and how their bodies grow.[9] Black and Latino children are two times more likely to go hungry than white children.[10]

A 2020 report by the Century Foundation, *Closing America's Education Funding Gaps*, showed that K–12 public schools are underfunded by nearly $150 billion each year, "robbing more than 30 million school children of the resources they need to succeed in the classroom."[11] Black and Latino children are the most under-resourced yet they're expected to meet the same standards as other students. In the workplace, instead of being recognized for the value they bring, mothers are often penalized for having children, frequently passed over for jobs and paid just 61.7 cents for every dollar earned by fathers.[12] For single mothers, low wages or unemployment can mean eating just one meal a day or going without antibiotics for a child's strep throat.

Sixty percent of formerly incarcerated people are jobless at any given time, and many of them are Black and Brown men who were living in poverty well before their convictions.[13] The jobs that they are able to secure are often in construction, waste management, or manufacturing. They are often severely underpaid, at constant risk of being terminated, and work in dangerous conditions. Children who live in poor-quality housing and low-income neighborhoods tend to have higher incidences of abuse and neglect and lower kindergarten readiness scores.[14] Poverty, which disproportionately affects Black, Latino, and Indigenous people, impacts health outcomes, causing higher rates of heart disease, diabetes, stroke, and other chronic conditions.[15] The CDC reports that Black women have the highest maternal mortality rate in the United States: 69.9 per 100,000 live births for 2021, nearly three times the rate of white women. A 2016 survey of white medical students revealed nearly half of them held false beliefs about Black patients, including biological differences such as thicker skin and less sensitive nerve endings.[16] A 2020 study found that Black babies are more likely to live in the care of a Black doctor.[17]

Coretta Scott King's last point—about our contempt rather than empathy for those experiencing poverty—is one of the main drivers of economic violence. A 2018 United Nations report conducted by an independent expert on extreme poverty and human rights found that America's preferred solution for extreme poverty is to criminalize and shame those in need of assistance: "For one of the world's wealthiest countries to have 40 million people living in poverty and over five million living in 'Third World' conditions is cruel and inhuman. . . . It seems driven primarily by contempt, and sometimes even by hatred for the poor, along with a 'winner takes all' mentality."[18]

This type of violence *sounds* different. It's a child's cries for formula that their mother can't afford. It's the crack in a father's voice as he asks for more time to pay the rent. It's a grandmother's muffled yelling in the next room from daily stress. It's the silence of a loved one who is never coming home again. These sounds of harm *should* haunt us, startle us to action, compel us to find a bravery and a courage we never knew we had. Instead there is no urgency. We look the other way. We blame families for their situations, and we question their appetite for success and the American dream.

About midway through the fall and spring semesters, Generation Hope hosts a half-day training for our Scholars and their mentors. To make it easier for Scholars to attend, we provide on-site childcare as well as breakfast, lunch, and snacks. At one of these trainings held in DC just a few years after I began the organization, a staff member approached me with a worried look on her face. Two little girls, the daughters of a Scholar, were stuffing bags of chips into their pockets and backpacks while the volunteers tended to the other children. We had been working with the young, single mother in her pursuit of an associate's degree at the University of the District of Columbia Community College, but we soon learned that the family of three was living in a homeless shelter. We said nothing that day. Instead, we ramped up our supports for her and her daughters and began making to-go boxes for every event, normalizing taking leftovers home. Sending everyone out the door with food in hand, just like at the end of Thanksgiving dinner, is now a hallmark of how we gather.

This story has a happy ending. That Scholar earned both her associate's and bachelor's degrees after eight and a half years navigating housing insecurity, apartment fires, and unemployment. With each milestone, we celebrated. In each challenge, we rallied. And while she and her children are doing well now, and she is working in a career she loves, the memory of her daughters and the snack bags serves as a constant reminder of the unreasonable request we make of parents in poverty. Navigate your life while hungry, houseless, in pain, stressed, without childcare, unemployed, and stigmatized. Work harder. Get a better-paying job. Get a promotion. Get an education.

Telling a mother whose children are perpetually hungry to just "get an education" reveals a significant blind spot: the cost of college puts it out of reach for those who need it most. Yes, a postsecondary credential offers life-changing benefits. College graduates are less likely to be unemployed than those with only a high school diploma, and on average, they earn $1 million more over their lifetimes.[19] Bachelor's degree holders are three and a half times less likely to be impoverished and nearly five times less likely to be imprisoned.[20] College graduates are also more likely to own their homes[21] and receive employer-provided retirement and health insurance benefits.[22] Research even suggests that they are more likely to eat dinner each night with their family.[23] But even with the long list of proven benefits—and the potential for more degrees to reduce economic disparities—higher education remains unaffordable for most families,[24] particularly for parents living in homeless shelters or working as cashiers for just $8.79 an hour.

In the early 1970s, Senator Claiborne Pell, a Democrat from Rhode Island, proposed a federal program for grants that would go directly to students, helping low- and moderate-income individuals access college. These funds would become the largest source of grants for higher education and the foundation of federal student aid in the US, making college more affordable for millions of students for the next several decades. When they were first distributed, during the 1972–73 academic year, Pell Grants reached about 170,000 students. In 1975, they covered nearly all (79 percent) of the average costs of tuition, fees, room, and board at public four-year colleges, which was $1,935 per year.[25] Fast-forward to 2017, when these grants covered just 29 percent of the same average costs because the total had skyrocketed to $20,770 per year.[26] The numbers are even more disparate at private institutions. In 1970, attending a private college cost about $3,000 per year. Today, the average cost is more than

$50,000 per year, but the maximum Pell Grant is only $7,395 annually.[27] Rising costs mean that the grant's purchasing power has been drastically weakened. Receiving a Pell Grant today no longer determines if you can afford college. It now covers only a small portion of the total bill, leaving recipients with the nearly impossible task of paying for the remaining expenses required to complete a degree. For the vast majority of teen parents, single parents, couples supporting a family with hourly jobs, grandparents raising grandchildren, and others living on the fringes, there are no reserves to pull from to pay for their education, no matter how smart or driven they are.

College tuition costs have risen at a higher rate of inflation than all other industries except hospital care.[28] Why has it become so expensive? Some attribute it to administrative bloat and campus amenities. In *After the Ivory Tower Falls: How College Broke the American Dream and Blew Up Our Politics—and How to Fix It*, Pulitzer Prize–winning journalist Will Bunch argues America's decision to treat higher education as a private not a public good is the main driver for increases. In other words, the amount of tax dollars going to public universities has plunged in most states, from 65 percent in the 1970s to 30 percent in 2013.[29] Schools pass those costs on to students and families who, in turn, must take out loans. During his presidency, Ronald Reagan led the charge to privatize college by slashing higher education spending, including $338 million of Pell Grants, and at the same time, lifting limits on borrowing money to pay tuition. Today, college, especially a four-year degree, has become an out-of-reach pathway to economic mobility. Americans are drowning in $1.6 trillion of student loan debt.[30] Unsurprisingly, at the epicenter of this crisis sits the same group that Reagan targeted with his welfare queen stereotype to justify cuts to public assistance programs—Black mothers. They hold higher amounts of student loan debt *than any other population*.

The improbability of college for parents in poverty is not just about the escalating costs of higher education, it's also about parents having to pay more to go to college than students who don't have children. In 2022, Generation Hope partnered with the Education Trust to release a report on college affordability and student parents. We found that out-of-pocket costs for a public college is two to five times higher for student parents than for their low-income peers without children.[31] In addition to tuition and fees, parents have to pay for childcare while they attend class, off-campus housing (most schools don't provide undergraduate family housing), transportation, medical expenses, and food for themselves and their children. A California Competes study found that student parents in the state pay $7,592 of out-of-pocket expenses annually on average on top of tuition and fees to attend college. Community colleges have lower tuition and fees, but costs can still add up. The same study found that parenting students in California receive more aid and scholarships from four-year institutions than from community colleges. Student parents at community colleges pay nearly $2,400 more annually than those at four-year institutions. This may not be the case in every community—the National College Attainment Network found that nationally 63 percent of community colleges are affordable for most students[32]—but it does illustrate how even community college student parents are feeling the crushing weight of neglect and underinvestment at these institutions.

Encouraging parents to work more so they can afford college isn't the answer either. In the US, nearly 30 percent of low-wage workers are logging more than forty hours per week, and 16 percent are working multiple jobs.[33] These jobs come with low pay that barely covers rent, often with unpredictable schedules, making it challenging to secure childcare or get to campus on time for class or meetings with professors. Our report with the Education Trust found that, on average, a student parent would need to work thirty to ninety hours per week to cover childcare and tuition costs at a public college or university in the US, leaving little time for studying, class, or their children. At Generation Hope, more than 70 percent of our Scholars work twenty or more hours a week in addition to attending school and caring for their children, and 35 percent work more than thirty hours a week. Hanging on to poorly paid jobs to keep your family afloat only to have those jobs block access to better opportunities to provide for your family is a vicious cycle.

Emerita, a young, single Latina mother in our first class of Scholars at Generation Hope, perfectly—and painfully—showed just how little margin under-resourced parents have in their daily lives. The daughter of immigrants from El Salvador, she joined our program in 2011 while juggling three jobs: a night manager at McDonald's, a front desk receptionist at a Catholic church, and an assembly-line worker building secure-line telephones. Despite working more than eighty hours a week—eighteen hours straight some days—she still managed to attend classes two days a week at Northern Virginia Community College, hoping to one day become a police officer or FBI agent. At home, her time was stretched even thinner. Emerita served as the primary translator for her parents, helped her four younger siblings with their homework, and contributed to the monthly bills. Behind her big brown eyes, peeking through her thick black curls, was a constant worry that she wasn't spending enough time with her three-year-old son, Dominic, and that exhaustion would cause her to fall asleep while driving between jobs and to and from campus. Her mentor, Kimberly, a former teen mother and now a successful business owner, often urged her to slow down and take care of herself. Emerita's response was always the same: "It's just me, so I have to work a million times as hard."

Emerita operated not only in a constant monetary deficit—her hourly wages eaten up by bills, gas for her commutes, college tuition, expenses for Dominic—but also in a relentless time deficit, juggling eighteen-hour work days, three hours of sleep, midterms, and a sick little one. Time poverty means not having enough hours in the day to maintain your physical and mental well-being, or if you're in college, to study and complete coursework. It's an acute problem for women, especially mothers, women of color, those without a college degree, and those with low income. In developed countries, women spend twice as many hours per day on unpaid work such as cooking, cleaning, and caring for children.[34] After gathering toys, washing dishes, balancing bills, making lunches, running baths, reading bedtime stories, and working one or more low-wage jobs, there simply aren't enough hours for another shift that pays little and would be mostly consumed by childcare costs. And if a mother or father is somehow able to enroll in college, research shows, on average, they have about 4.3 hours less per week for studying than students without children, even those also working several jobs.[35]

If working more hours isn't a viable strategy for parents to afford college, then why not just apply for scholarships to foot the bill? When teen parents are accepted into Generation Hope's program, they often tell us how shocked they were to find financial support for college that not only accommodated their parenting status but required it. That's because, traditionally, scholarships carry stipulations that tend to exclude parents, like the need to enroll full-time, live on campus, study abroad for a semester, fall under a certain age, or attend a four-year school. Very few scholarships specifically support mothers and fathers, and even fewer recognize juggling multiple jobs, patching together childcare, and feeding a family of three on fifty dollars a week as indicators of leadership and success. The difficulty also lies in the likelihood of receiving a scholarship. In 2016, $6.1 billion in scholarships was awarded to 1.58 million students, including four hundred different United Negro College Fund scholarships, $20,000 awards from the Coca-Cola Foundation, and TheDream.US scholarships for undocumented immigrant youth. While these investments can be life-changing for recipients, only 7 percent of college students receive scholarships each year,[36] with an average award of around $4,200. Just 0.1 percent of undergraduate students receive $25,000 or more in scholarship money.[37]

For more affluent families in America, the path to higher education looks completely different. Upper-class students not only have the funds to pay for college debt-free; they also benefit from systems and practices that lower costs and remove hurdles to enrollment and completion. Merit-based scholarships, which don't consider financial need, often go to students from well-resourced backgrounds, with families that can afford the pricey tutors and college prep programs that boost GPAs and standardized test scores. As a result, college ends up being *less expensive* for them. These families are also twice as likely to send their children to elite colleges, which offer more generous scholarships, helped by robust social networks and legacy admissions that favor applicants with family ties to the school.[38] Low-income students, on the other hand, are more likely to attend underfunded schools, such as community colleges and HBCUs, which offer less financial aid and have been historically neglected. Students of color are more vulnerable to predatory for-profit colleges that promise fast-track credentials and high earnings. Thirteen percent of Black students enroll in these schools, compared to just 4 percent of white students.[39] A mind-boggling 75 percent of Black students at for-profit schools who leave without a degree end up defaulting on their loans.[40] Meanwhile, wealthier students avoid loans entirely and don't have to work during school, giving them time to focus on academics, get extra help from professors, and participate in on- and off-campus opportunities that enrich their résumés and boost their postgraduation job prospects.

Federal systems also make college more affordable and accessible for wealthier students. America's richest families saw their wealth jump 25 percent in 2019, bringing their collective fortune to a massive $5.9 trillion. By 2023, despite a global pandemic that ravaged ordinary households, the number of American billionaires grew from 614 to 737. Tax breaks for the rich, like not having to report sizable chunks of their income, have only widened the wealth gap and further limited opportunities to make college more affordable for the average family, particularly Black and Latino families. In 2019, Senator Elizabeth Warren of Massachusetts called for broad debt cancellation and universal free college through an Ultra-Millionaire Tax, a 2 percent annual tax on the seventy-five thousand families holding $50 million or more in wealth. The plan was estimated to give every American the chance to attend a two- or four-year public college for free. If this seems unrealistic, billionaire Facebook (now Meta) founder Mark Zuckerberg saw a $27.3 billion increase in his wealth in 2019. That increase alone is more than seven times the combined endowments of all HBCUs in this country[41] and would be enough to cover more than a third of the annual estimated cost needed to eliminate tuition at every US public college and university.[42] That's just his 2019 *increase* in wealth, not his total wealth, which is estimated at $113.5 billion.[43]

College affordability has always been solvable. We can look to the American High School movement—a push for mass secondary education in the early twentieth century—as a template. The movement made high school available to not just elite wealthy students who had historically paid for their education but to average families. It was driven largely by small communities across the country that saw the economic value and broader importance of investing in young people's education. They were willing to pay taxes to build public schools, a commitment that transformed people's lives, bolstered the middle class, and advanced the US as a world leader. Today, there are 23,519 public high schools in the US and little debate about whether high school should be free.[44] We can do the same for college, but there must be a recognition in the value of investing in the education and career opportunities of all people, including parents.

Dr. King's solution wasn't pushing families to work more, urging them to apply for more assistance, slashing safety net programs, or giving tax breaks to the rich. His nonviolent agenda focused on what we most often remember—the sit-ins of Black protestors at diner counters despite being shouted at and dragged to the floor, and the bus boycotts in Montgomery, Alabama, where tens of thousands of Black residents walked, carpooled, or biked for more than a year. Dr. King's agenda also demanded action to improve the plight of America's poorest families: Employing more Black Americans, making it more difficult for employers to discriminate against them by bolstering their collective power. Transforming unions by purging them of racist and discriminatory practices, uniting people to advocate for important protections, higher pay, and so on, as he did for the sanitation workers in Memphis. Ensuring voting rights for Black Americans and marginalized populations, giving them the ability to influence legislation, appointments to the Supreme Court, and more. Enacting guaranteed income, providing unconditional, recurring cash payments to assist families with housing, food, medical care, childcare, dramatically reducing poverty and increasing access to opportunities like higher education. This was—and remains—the proper response to economic violence. These are the spaces where we must find the bravery, courage, and fearlessness to stop it.

Right now, more than four million undergraduate college students across the country are parenting. Two-thirds of them are living at or near the federal poverty line, like Emerita was. Over thirty million more smart, hardworking mothers and fathers are shackled by low-wage jobs that keep them from even considering college. Marginal increases in federal aid and a few more scholarships won't create the seismic shift needed to put a college degree within their reach. Thankfully, Dr. King, Coretta Scott King, and the Poor People's Campaign championed many of the same investments and reforms we must fight for today. In addition to more jobs and guaranteed income, we need an increased minimum wage, expanded Pell Grants, student loan forgiveness, and free tuition at public colleges and universities. We need K–12 and postsecondary programs that address racial and socioeconomic disparities; strengthened college preparation for under-resourced students; universal pre-K and affordable childcare; emergency financial grants to students in crisis;

significant investments in community colleges, HBCUs, minority serving institutions (MSIs), and tribal colleges and universities (TCUs). All of these policy solutions, along with others, would have major impacts on parents' ability to pursue and earn a college degree. These are our opportunities to *do something*.

Each day, we make history, either by listening for the hurt and pain that surrounds us or by just folding it into the daily rhythm of our lives. Perhaps the most deafening sound of violence is stillness: the sound of no one doing anything at all to stop it. Whether we act or not, violence exists—in all its forms—even when it's dressed up in persuasive rhetoric or wrapped in catchy phrases and harmonies. True courage is peeling back the comfortable explanations and dealing with the hard, ugly truth at the messy core. Bravery is the act of closing our eyes and seeing with our hearts what is right in front of us. Fearlessness is pushing for reform even in the face of enraged mobs, threats, risks, and the misconception that by making life better for others we somehow lose something for ourselves.

CHAPTER 5

CHILDCARE AND BREATHING

Something sweet and beautiful can come from the most desperate and dark places, from sheer necessity and primal protection. The origins of the ubiquitous Native American food, fry bread, can be traced back 160 years to the Long Walk, a three-hundred-mile journey to exile for thousands of Diné (Navajo) people from their homelands to New Mexico's Bosque Redondo Reservation. Tired hands rolled the puffy crisp bread together from sparse ingredients provided by the US government during this uprooting—flour, salt, sugar, and lard—to fend off starvation. The emotional potency of American blues music emerged from oppressed Black communities in the rural Deep South after the Civil War. Descendants of enslaved people detailed their subjugation and suffering through songs of longing, loss, and desire, drawing on African origins, field hollers sung on the plantation, spirituals, and country string ballads. Economic downturn and increasing racial conflict during the 1920s and 1930s spearheaded the Social Realism art movement. Through murals, paintings, and sculptures, artists including José Clemente Orozco, Diego Rivera, and Elizabeth Catlett depicted the deteriorating conditions of the poor and working classes, challenged oppressive systems, and called for justice and freedom. Catlett, an American-born Mexican artist known for her sculptures and prints of African American women, described the necessity of her creations: "Art is only important to the extent that it aids in the liberation of our people."[1]

By no means is desperation the preferred muse, but it's the muse we're given. While it has sparked tribal traditions, music genres, and artistic movements, on an individual level, it has forced mothers and fathers with scant resources to create makeshift toys, recipes from bare cabinets, and summer vacations out of a day at the park. Intertwined with poverty are the ingenious ways that parents are forced to meet their children's needs, shield suffering and struggle, and invent enriching experiences despite having so little.

Summers in Williamsburg are hot and muggy. The humidity clings to your body like another layer of clothing. As a toddler, during these months, Nerissa would beg me for the cool relief of running through the sprinkler or jumping in a pool. Water Country USA, Virginia's largest water park, was just minutes from our campus apartment, full of 1950s and 1960s surf-themed rides that gushed refreshing water over giggling kids. But as a single teen mother, I couldn't afford a day at the water park or even a pool pass. Living in a dorm meant I didn't have a yard for cartwheels through a sprinkler. Instead, we waited for the bursts of rain that would suddenly take hold of summer afternoons. At the first hint of a darkened sky, we'd sprint to the window, then hurry down the stairs and out the door of our building with our arms open wide, welcoming the raindrops on our faces and eventually all over. We danced. We held hands. We investigated the worms on the ground. But mostly, we laughed, the sound of our joy mingling with the quiet afternoon shower.

We forget how good a single drop of rain can feel on our skin. If we surrender to it—tipping our heads back, closing our eyes, inviting the taste of the clouds and the stars on our tongue—we can come alive.

I don't think Nerissa remembers the pool membership I couldn't afford or the nearby waterpark never within reach, mostly because every day I tried to create experiences that shielded her from how precarious things were. She had no idea how insufficient I felt or how much I worried that my inability to provide her with the things that other children had might create a lasting imprint on her life for which I was wholly responsible. What anchored me was her smile—her smile in the midst of a rain shower was brighter than even the sun. I liked to believe that those bursts of light would be enough for both of us.

The most suffocating experiences of my life were unrelated to the asthma I was diagnosed with at three years old and rarely took place in medical settings. These solitary moments could take place anywhere, at any time, without warning. I can't count all of the times as a young mother I felt like I couldn't breathe, when life caught hold of me and dragged me down into its undertow. They were too frequent. An eviction notice taped to my apartment door. A phone call from my daughter's father from the county jail in the early hours of the morning. My white station wagon stranded on the side of the highway, cars rushing past me and my little girl. The crises crashed in, submerging me in urgency and shock. While in each of those instances, I went through the motions—answering questions or nodding my head or doing what needed to be done—all the while, I wasn't really *breathing*.

The day we were forced to leave Nerissa's childcare center I couldn't breathe. The director's face was soft, as it usually was when she greeted us in the hallway during morning drop-off or watched over giggling little ones on the playground until parents arrived in the afternoons, but that day, after she explained that Nerissa couldn't stay enrolled, her lips came together in an immovable, matter-of-fact expression. We stood there, the weight of her words landing differently on both of us. I tried to inhale, but there wasn't enough air for me to take in. My legs felt numb, as if detached from the rest of my body. In my breathlessness, I searched for the right words, but there really weren't any *right* words.

I was late again on the monthly tuition payments at the campus childcare center, and while the director knew that unlike the rest of the parents, mostly professors and college administrators, I was an undergraduate student parent, she had motioned me over to where she stood outside of her office one sunny afternoon to tell me I'd have to withdraw Nerissa from the center. There would be no more extensions, no more special payment plans. Our time there had come to an end. She allowed us a few more days, long enough for Nerissa's teachers to put together an album of laminated construction paper bound together with bows of blue yarn to document some of her special moments at the school—proudly holding a frenzied finger painting, a wagon full of dressed-up toddlers heading across campus in the Halloween parade, her and her friends bundled up in winter coats and hats posing in front of the swings with wide smiles. We packed the album along with her nap blanket, sippy cup, and changes of clothes in a bag, and we left. As we drove down the wooded driveway, the center getting smaller and smaller in the distance, Nerissa asked why she had to say good-bye to her friends and teachers. I didn't have the right words or enough air to breathe.

Back in 2002, I was a junior in college, taking out loans to pay $800 a month for Nerissa to attend the Williamsburg Campus Child Care (WCCC) center while shouldering a full course load at William & Mary and working part-time where I could. A couple years earlier, I enrolled Nerissa at WCCC with the help of a scholarship that partly covered her monthly tuition, but after one year, the scholarship funds ran out, and I was forced to pay the full rate. I tried to cover what I could and asked for more time to take care of the rest while racking up late charges. Childcare was just one of my many bills among rent, medical co-pays, prescriptions, groceries, gas and car maintenance, car insurance, my college books and tuition, and more. I was a master at intricate daily calculations for allocating a small amount of funds across competing expenses with the ultimate goal of keeping Nerissa clothed, fed, and housed. The calculations rarely resulted in an easy answer. There was always a sacrifice—or many sacrifices. That day, it was WCCC.

Losing childcare had major implications for my ability to continue in college, but my biggest concern that day wasn't about my own education, it was about Nerissa's. WCCC was the one experience I could give her that wasn't lacking. In our two-bedroom apartment, our heat didn't always work, the cabinets and fridge were sometimes nearly bare, and our furniture was sparse and falling apart. My Subaru station wagon was leaking oil, and the mechanic kept reminding me that one day, no matter how much oil we poured in, it wouldn't make it home. I couldn't afford to sign Nerissa up for enriching activities like dance or swim classes. WCCC, a beautiful, white 6,500-square-foot building with seven classrooms, a large multipurpose room, kitchen, offices, and outdoor playgrounds—all specifically designed for young children—was the one thing in Nerissa's life that was *abundant*. Large windows poured sunshine into brightly colored learning areas full of stimulating toys and books while kind, caring teachers provided individualized attention to each child. I worried about whether I'd have enough money to buy her new sneakers or birthday cupcakes for class, but I never worried about whether Nerissa was receiving a high-quality early education. And now, because I had failed, it was gone.

To say something is broken is to say that it was once whole. But many things come into existence fractured or missing something, inadequate, disjointed. We're taught that systems begin on the right footing, crafted with good intentions and proper supports, and time and neglect erode the strong inner workings and cause cracks to form. But what if the cracks were always there? "Make the world a better place" may sound like a call to get things back on track, but many times, it is a call to create a new track with a new destination—to right wrongs, to fix things never meant to be just or fair, and to remedy holes and gaps.

Childcare in America is not currently a broken system; it's a system that *began* broken. It's functioning as it was designed; to fix it, we need to reimagine it. Without childcare, parents can't go to work or school, children lose out on early learning experiences during their most formative years, and our economy suffers. Childcare is the lifeblood of society, but it is severely flawed, devalued, and deprioritized. While nearly all families struggle to afford and access quality childcare, these challenges hit families with low income more acutely. Almost 40 percent of families earning less than $50,000 per year spend more than $18,000 on childcare annually. That's a staggering 36 percent of household income.[2] The crisis is a tangled mix of factors: childcare is an expensive service due to its labor-intensive nature and need for low teacher-to-child ratio, there is insufficient public funding, the workforce is poorly paid, and there are many misconceptions—that early childhood providers lack professional skills and that childcare is a personal albatross rather than a collective responsibility. But to understand childcare's broken origins, we have to go back to the beginning of the early care and education industry in America.

The boom of English colonization in North America in the early 1600s began with a colony called Jamestown in Chesapeake Bay in 1607. In time, the Plymouth Company reorganized as the Council for New England (1620), the Dutch West India Company (1621), the Company of New France (1627), and the Massachusetts Bay Company (1629) brought thousands of colonists, many with families and indentured servants, to North America. Colonists were drawn by the promise of massive land grants. Lord Baltimore offered one hundred acres to every free married man who paid his own way to Maryland, plus another one thousand to two thousand acres for bringing five or more people. This land belonged to the original inhabitants of North America, who numbered more than five million before Europeans invaded its shores.[3] In order for white colonists to gain control and reap the economic gains, they exploited, raped, and murdered the Indigenous people. They also needed free labor to build colonies and exploit the natural resources, which came in the form of indentured servants—mostly poor Europeans, manipulated and abused Native Americans, and kidnapped and enslaved Africans.

The year 1619 marks the beginning of African slavery in the continental British colonies. That's when a privateer, *The White Lion*, brought approximately twenty Africans to Jamestown, Virginia, trading them as slaves for food. By 1675, slavery was a well-established system in the colonies. By 1700, enslaved people had essentially replaced indentured servants, and by 1860, "the nearly 4 million American slaves were worth some $3.5 billion, making them the largest single financial asset in the entire US economy, worth more than all manufacturing and railroads combined."[4] This forced and unpaid labor primarily took place on the tobacco, rice, and indigo plantations along the southern coast, from when the sun rose in the morning until it set in the evening, toiling for as much as fourteen hours each day. Men and women worked in the fields clearing land, planting seeds, and harvesting crops, and in the plantation house cooking meals, tending to the fires, and washing clothes and linens. In the house, they also served as caregivers. Enslaved African women were often the nanny or "nurse" of their oppressor's children, even breastfeeding them, with no agency to care for their own, unable to protect them from violence, feed them properly, or prevent them from being sold away.

The inherent brokenness of childcare in America comes from being born out of chattel slavery—a system legally supported by the United States and Europe that considered people, mostly Africans and Black Americans, and their children as property that could be bought, sold, and owned, *forever*. As the original primary childcare providers for colonist families, enslaved African women were treated as property, never valued or fairly compensated for their labor, never respected for their skills and abilities. These sentiments would become the underpinnings of the early care and education industry in America. Even after the Thirteenth Amendment to the US Constitution abolished slavery in 1865, Black women were confined to domestic jobs, many working as childcare providers for white families. The pay was insufficient, the days were excruciatingly long, and they rarely saw their own children. In 1912, the *Independent* published a Black mother's account of working fourteen to sixteen hours a day as a "nurse" for just ten dollars a week, allowed to go home only twice a month: "Whether in the cook kitchen, at the washtub, over the sewing machine, behind the baby carriage, or at the ironing board, we are but little more than pack horses, beasts of burden, slaves!"[5]

Today, 94 percent of childcare workers are female, and 40 percent are people of color.[6] One in five childcare workers are Black women, though they're only 7 percent of the overall workforce.[7] Regardless of their education level, Black childcare providers earn an average of seventy-eight cents less per hour than white providers.[8] Even before COVID-19 resulted in the closing of nearly sixteen thousand childcare centers,[9] childcare workers were among the lowest-paid workers in the nation.[10] According to a report by the Education Trust and the US Chamber of Commerce Foundation, "53 percent of childcare workers' families were enrolled in at least one public assistance program (such as the Supplemental Nutrition Assistance Program and the Temporary Assistance for Needy Families), compared to 21 percent of the families of the nation's workforce as a whole." In 2018, women working full-time, year-round in the childcare industry earned a median of $29,900, with Black women earning $27,000 and Latina women only $22,074.[11] In addition to earning low wages, childcare providers, as hourly workers, rarely receive employer-sponsored benefits. Only 15 percent of childcare workers have health insurance through their job, compared with 49.9 percent of workers in other industries.[12] These numbers aren't accidental or simply the effects of neglect over time. They represent the lasting impacts of an industry that grew out of America's brutal legacy of slavery.

Wilma Mankiller—the first female principal chief of the Cherokee Nation, the first woman elected as chief of a major Native tribe, and an advocate for youth who expanded the Head Start program for Cherokee children—once said: "I learned a long time ago that I can't control the challenges the creator sends my way, but I can control the way I think about them and deal with them." Ensuring all families have access to economic mobility and wealth building isn't about controlling whether or not challenges like low wages, racism, and sexism come their way. We have limped along with these challenges for a long time. But we do have the ability to acknowledge them, be honest about how they came to be, and uproot them.

We have inherited a *diseased* childcare system. We can't change the immoral seeds from which it sprouted or its twisted and scarred branches that have now propagated across the country, but we can change the way we view, understand, and deal with the system. Naming its ugly origins prevents us from underestimating how significant and engrained the problems are and encourages us to seek out completely new ways of solving them. Pathways to upward mobility for mothers and fathers, like securing a higher-paying job or going back to school, aren't possible without a quality childcare system that is both accessible and affordable. To achieve that, providers—many of them parents themselves—need to earn fair and family-sustaining wages. And childcare facilities and families need subsidies that lower the cost of childcare.

How are families navigating astronomical childcare prices? In 2023, Generation Hope released a report on the childcare experiences of our students in the DC area, a place with the country's most expensive center-based infant care, averaging $419 a week. The report illuminated the significant care barrier for young parents who want to earn a post-secondary credential.[13] The majority of respondents were mothers of color and first-generation college students parenting children under the age of four. While the assumption might be that a parent in college is accessing formal, center-based childcare in order to work and attend class, the reality is, this type of care is often too expensive. The majority (71 percent) of our respondents (82 percent of whom were making less than $30,000 annually) relied on informal or unpaid childcare, including family, friends, neighbors, or public school programs. There are benefits to family, friends, and neighbors providing care, such as more individualized attention and lower costs, but there are also downsides, such as disruptions in care when a family member gets sick or a neighbor moves out of state. These disruptions can keep parents from showing up to work and from getting to class, which means less money and falling behind academically. Another concern is the quality of informal care, which might not include an educational curriculum. But going without childcare—informal or not—isn't an option. Sixty percent[14] of parenting students are working full-time in addition to attending college so childcare is an absolute necessity.

This patching together of care isn't unique to our Scholars. It mirrors the forced creativity of families across the country. About 61 percent of parents with at least one child under the age of seventeen said they don't have any formal childcare arrangements, and the percentage is higher for lower-income households. Sixty-seven percent of parents with annual household incomes under $50,000 do not utilize formal childcare, compared to 52 percent of households earning more than $200,000. As income goes up, so does enrollment in daycare centers, preschools, and before and aftercare programs.[15] For families trying to make ends meet each day, formal care is just too expensive. According to Care.com's *2025 Cost of Care Report*, the average weekly cost of formal childcare is $321, up 13 percent from $284 in 2022. The average cashier takes home $591 a week,[16] and the average janitor takes home $697 a week.[17] Tuition costs for a formal daycare center would eat up 54 percent and 46 percent of their weekly salaries, respectively, leaving very little for rent, food, transportation, clothes, medicine, and other necessities. Like our Scholars, many parents are forced to rely on partners, relatives, friends, or neighbors to provide stints of care for their little ones, strung together by complicated, delicate plans for getting them from one house to another.

And while formal childcare is too expensive for most parents, it's also too expensive for most institutions to operate. When my staff and I talk to college leaders about student parents, childcare is often the first thing that comes up, immediately followed by a proclamation of how expensive it is to build and sustain childcare centers. And they're right. Start-up expenditures for franchised centers range from $59,000 to $3 million, not including the ongoing costs of commercial space, payroll, licensing, insurance, food, and equipment. Most institutions don't have the data on their student-parent population to justify these costs. Under-resourced schools like community colleges and minority-serving institutions have tight budgets that make childcare difficult to cover. Exorbitant costs have resulted in few schools across the country offering on-campus childcare, and many that once did have been forced to close them down. Even before the childcare crisis peaked during the pandemic, the number of public higher education institutions with childcare services had been declining for years—dropping 14 percentage points, from 59 percent in 2004 to 45 percent in 2019, with community colleges, the schools most accessible to parents, seeing the steepest decline of nearly 17 percentage points.[18] And even if an institution has a childcare center on campus, without intentional policies and investments, they are likely to enroll mostly faculty and staff children due to costs, long waiting lists, age restrictions, and operating hours.

Marian Wright Edelman, author and founder of the Children's Defense Fund, once said, "Children don't vote, but adults who do must stand up and vote for them." Throughout America's history, not enough adults have stood up and voted for children, including their right to a quality early childhood education. Despite 74 percent of voters supporting more federal funding for childcare and early learning programs,[19] Congress allowed $24 billion in pandemic-related childcare subsidies to expire in September 2024, forcing many centers to close and families to scramble for care. Compared to other countries, the US spends an abysmal 0.2 percent of its GDP on childcare for little ones under the age of two, which comes out to about $200 a year in an annual tax credit for most families who pay for childcare. The average percentage of GDP spent on childcare for toddlers in other wealthy countries in the Organization for Economic Cooperation and Development (OECD) is 0.7 percent, primarily in the form of subsidized childcare.[20] Denmark spends $23,140 annually per child on care for those two and under—more than a hundred times America's investment. In November 2023, the Biden administration proposed a $16 billion investment to help stabilize the childcare sector.[21] In March 2024, the final funding package for the fiscal year included $1 billion for childcare and early learning programs. Incremental increases in funding for childcare won't solve this problem.

When it comes to campus-based solutions, which has the potential to make college a reality for more parents, the federal Child Care Access Means Parents in School (CCAMPIS) grants program administered by the US Department of Education provides funds to colleges to help their low-income student parents pay for accredited, licensed childcare on or off campus. In 2021, the average CCAMPIS award was $157,000,[22] and over the years, its funding has increased from $16 million to $51 million. Still, the Institute for Women's Policy Research estimates that CCAMPIS only reaches about eleven thousand student parents—a mere 1 percent of students who could benefit from it nationwide, just a drop in the bucket. Campus-based childcare solutions are few and far between. When we asked our DC-area students about campus-based childcare, 92 percent didn't have access to or were unaware of on-campus childcare options, and 78 percent wished their campuses did more to support their childcare needs.

Beyond college campuses, the main source of public funding for childcare is the federal Child Care and Development Fund (CCDF). This program helps low-income families pay for childcare through vouchers. However, the funding is insufficient. Only a small fraction of eligible children receive help, and many families who need it don't qualify. According to the National Women's Law Center, a family of three with an income above $43,440 a year in 2020 couldn't qualify for vouchers in thirty-three states. The program also doesn't fully cover the cost of care, especially for infants and toddlers, incentivizing providers to prioritize slots for parents who can pay out of pocket and leading to low teacher pay to offset costs.

A more affordable alternative to center-based childcare is home childcare. These providers care for small groups of children in their private homes, a model that keeps costs down for families and creates entrepreneurial opportunities, particularly for women of color. Tuition rates for in-home childcare are approximately 30 percent less than center-based childcare, partly because of lower overhead costs.[23] According to the National Survey of Early Care and Education (NSECE), in the United States, there are one million paid providers—40 percent of them people of color—caring for three million children from newborn to age five in their homes. Approximately 118,000 of these providers are licensed, regulated, exempt from licensure, or registered.[24] They have been deeply impacted by America's devaluing of childcare. Lack of resources, visibility, steady income and benefits, and supportive policies have forced many home childcare providers out of business. Between 2005 and 2017, more than ninety thousand licensed home childcare businesses closed their doors, significantly affecting children's early learning and parents' ability to work or attend school, particularly for lower-income families, those with children under four, and Hispanic or Black families who more often rely on home or family childcare.[25] Home childcare providers and the families they serve feel the childcare crisis acutely. But Jessica Sager, cofounder and CEO of All Our Kin, a nonprofit that invests in home childcare solutions, reminds us that it doesn't have to be this way: "Affordability for families and compensation for educators don't have to exist in opposition. They're really part of the same thing: a publicly funded system that allows families to afford care and allows educators to earn fair wages."

When I was a mom in college, and I lost childcare at WCCC, I was lucky enough to find a federally funded solution. As a teen mother, I learned early on that keeping a catalog of contingency plans, written down or in a constant rotation in my head, was vital. As much as I loved the care Nerissa received at WCCC, I knew our time there was coming to an end long before the conversation outside of the director's office that day. So I had started researching other options months earlier. It turned out that because Nerissa was now a toddler, she qualified for Williamsburg's Head Start program. After voice mails, piles of paperwork, prayers, and hope that everything would fall into place in time for the start of the fall semester, I received the call that she had been accepted into the program. I went from paying $800 a month to $35 a month. Without Head Start, there's a good chance I would never have graduated from college.

Head Start is a federal early childhood program that promotes school readiness for children in families with low income by offering educational, nutritional, health, and social services. In 2019, Congress authorized more than $10 billion for Head Start, which serves about one million children annually.[26] While the numbers may seem large, the 49,992 Head Start and Early Head Start classrooms across the country still fall short of meeting the care needs of all eligible children. In addition to capacity, accessibility is also an issue. Head Start programs, which differ from state to state and county to county, don't always align with where child poverty is most concentrated.

In other words, many of the communities that need Head Start programs the most either don't have them or face long waiting lists.[27] For those children who are able to enroll in Head Start, like Nerissa, research shows positive long-term impacts. A Georgetown University study found that Head Start students in Tulsa, Oklahoma, performed better in middle school math and were more likely to advance to the next grade in elementary and middle school.[28] Another study, by the Hamilton Project at the Brookings Institution, found that Head Start students were more likely to graduate from high school, attend college, and earn a postsecondary degree, license, or certification.[29] The National Head Start Association found that participants are 12 percent less likely to live in poverty as adults and 29 percent less likely to receive public assistance.[30]

The last few years have brought recognition that a childcare crisis exists, and with that recognition has come important investments and creative solutions, some of which make going to college as a parent easier. In 2024, the National Head Start Association partnered with the Association of Community College Trustees to create a five-year Kids On Campus Initiative, which aims to bring more Head Start programs to community colleges nationwide, providing qualifying student parents with free, high-quality childcare and early education for their families. In 2019 and 2023, my organization worked with Senator Cory Booker of New Jersey on the Preparing and Resourcing Our Student Parents and Early Childhood Teachers (PROSPECT) Act. It would have increased access to affordable, quality infant and toddler childcare for student parents at community colleges and minority-serving institutions and provided training to infant and toddler childcare talent by investing $9 billion over five years. State-level innovations are also happening that make childcare more accessible for mothers and fathers who want to go to college. In 2022, Georgia announced student parents would be considered a "priority group" for receiving financial assistance through the Childcare and Parent Services (CAPS) program, which helps pay for childcare for families with no to low incomes so they can work or attend school. These efforts show that progress is possible. Large-scale change will require significant increases in funding, different ways of thinking about the value of childcare and early childhood educators, and a recognition of the deeply embedded inequities in our childcare system.

My mother keeps a children's book, *Tar Beach* by painter Faith Ringgold, on her bookshelf. In brightly colored, quilt-like illustrations, Ringgold tells the story of Cassie Louise Lightfoot, a little Black girl in Harlem in the 1930s who goes up to the tar-paper roof of her family's apartment building and transforms it into a sparkling beach on the hot summer days in the city. She dreams of taking flight from the shores of Tar Beach over the crowded skyline to escape the harsh realities that shape her life—her family doesn't have much money, her mother often cries, and her father comes home tired and worn out from long shifts as a construction worker on bridges and skyscrapers. Cassie's flights are often about righting wrongs—like soaring over the union building that denies her father entry because he's Black and then buying it for him—and sometimes they're delightful excursions, like wearing the George Washington Bridge "like a giant diamond necklace." In every instance, she creates a very different existence: "Sleeping on Tar Beach was magical. Lying on the roof in the night, with stars and skyscraper buildings all around me, made me feel rich, like I owned all that I could see." In a 1991 *New York Times* review, novelist Rosellen Brown points out that Ringgold's story is both whimsical and painful: "a beguiling promise that turns worse into better, and a deprivation into an advantage. It's a habit of artists as well as poor people."

It's tempting to romanticize Tar Beach or fry bread or a child sitting at the feet of their mother in a college classroom or a dance in a summer rainstorm, but Brown reminds us that these sweet and beautiful things, born from desperation and limitation, are a means of *survival*. They are the fruits of trees that are rarely watered, rarely given sun. They are magic from nothing. They are innovations and maneuvers to prevent our babies from the lasting effects of want and need. Carving out a better life for our children requires affordable, quality childcare, but too often, that feels as improbable as climbing to the top of the tallest building in New York City, spreading our arms wide, and taking flight.

The world would be a much more dazzling and breathtaking place if families could instead craft, innovate, and exist out of *abundance* and *liberation*. Imagine if running through sprinklers, jumping in pools, and burying toes deep in the sand were real possibilities for *all children* on sweltering summer days. Think of the learning and brilliance that would come from every toddler sitting in brightly colored classrooms with well-paid teachers and plenty of books and learning stations. Consider the trajectory of families if parents could afford reliable care to pursue their own education and to one day work in fulfilling careers that actually pay the bills and help create generational wealth.

Until we get there, a diseased system means families are suffocating, breathing is a luxury, each day is a gut punch, one crisis unfolding after another. Lack of childcare becomes the reason to stay in a graveyard shift, delay enrolling in college, and feel like you're failing your child. It is a heaviness that sits on our chest, leaving us susceptible to the strong undertow of deprivation and oppression, keeping our dreams just out of reach.

It was in a preschool classroom at the Episcopal church that my children learned the art of breathing. They came home eager to teach me the downward dog, the tree, and the butterfly, proudly holding their slightly shaking toddler bodies in each pose in our living room. With their movements, they intentionally controlled their breaths and showed me how to finish by gently placing a hand on their heart. All these years later, despite being in a different place in my life and in my parenting journey, I still have to remind myself to breathe deeply—to stop in moments of crisis and to inhale the thickness of the air. But my children's full breaths tenderly whisper to me the words of poet Nayyirah Waheed: "be softer with you. you are a breathing thing."

CHAPTER 6

TRANSPORTATION AND WHAT FOLLOWS

The silence of the early morning is deceptively peaceful. The earth hasn't fully opened its eyes, and we're just guests in its sluggish, blue, dewy haze. This was about the time I would leave my apartment in Newport News, Virginia, to drop my infant daughter off at her aunt's house and head to campus during my freshman year of college. In the quiet, matinal hours, I made multiple trips from the apartment to my boyfriend's gray 1976 Cadillac—first with the diaper bag, then with a backpack full of books, notebooks, and lactation supplies, and then with my baby in her car seat, her little brown eyes trying to discern my face in the sun's pink hue just beginning to break through the sky above.

Playing the one Baby Einstein CD of classical music that someone had given me, I set out on the road, tensely gripping the steering wheel. I'd have to remind myself that no matter how hard I held on to it, we may not make it to each destination on time, or at all. My roundtrip commute to campus was 150 miles, from Newport News to Portsmouth to Williamsburg and then back again, in the evening during the height of rush hour. There were so many variables. My boyfriend had to let me use his car—I didn't get my own until a few months into my freshman year—and he often took it without telling me or withheld it when we got into arguments. The car had to be working, and it was constantly in the shop for oil leaks and overheating. I needed enough gas to make the long journey, and we were barely able to pay rent and keep enough food in the house. Traffic was dense on the long, tree-lined stretch of I-64 and in the Hampton Roads Bridge Tunnel, sometimes making my total driving time three to four hours. With no other transportation or housing options, there was nothing peaceful about these rides. I spent them worrying about not making it through college simply because of how hard it was to make it *to* college.

That early morning drive wasn't optional. If I didn't find a way to campus, even in the most unreasonable circumstances, I might never escape the run-down apartment complex we were living in and all of the run-down apartment complexes I could see in our future. I was young, but struggling through the previous couple of years had taught me an unspoken truth about upward mobility: our capacity to earn more money, further our education, and connect with people who can open doors for us hinges upon physically getting from one place to another. What may seem simple for some—a working car in the driveway, a full tank of gas, a bike ride to the subway station, a stroll across campus from the dorm room to class—is a backbreaking task for others. Parents with few resources, parents who are navigating all that I was as a young mother and more, are less stagnated by their lack of talent or drive than their inability to access places that amplify and build on their skills and potential. No matter how hard they try, most will never make it to these places.

Thick, crimson-colored lines barreling through swaths of land with the sole purpose of division, impediment, hoarding, and oppression. Whether you were allowed to raise a family inside or outside those arbitrary shapes determined your ability to get a good-paying job, to breathe clean air, to send your children to quality schools, to access prenatal care, to run through a park, and so on. Sometimes it was a difference of just a thousand feet or one or two blocks to the left or right, but these boundaries cemented the undeniable fact that place *mattered*. And it still does.

Redlining and segregation were codified by the Federal Housing Administration (FHA) at its inception in 1934 by policies that legally denied mortgages in and near Black neighborhoods, marked on maps of US metropolitan areas by distinct and formidable red shaded configurations. Outside of these areas, the FHA was subsidizing large subdivisions for white people. This state-sponsored discriminatory practice was predicated on a baseless theory that providing loans to Black people was too risky and would lead to declining property values. In reality, Black families purchasing homes in all-white or mostly white neighborhoods actually increased overall property values, because with so little supply, they often paid more for their homes.[1] But facts and evidence weren't necessary to justify these damaging policies—just fear.

In President Franklin D. Roosevelt's promising 1932 New Deal platform, there was no mention of the damaging impacts that would come from many of its key programs. Redlining was among several of the administration's efforts, including Social Security and the National Labor Relations Act, that would systematically oppress people of color. During the 1934 Democratic National Convention in Chicago, Roosevelt inspired listeners: "Throughout the Nation, men and women, forgotten in the political philosophy of the Government of the last years, look to us here for guidance and for more equitable opportunity to share in the distribution of national wealth." But for America's most destitute families, these empty words never amounted to additional jobs, better pay, stable housing, or more food on the table. Their extended hands never received any distribution of national wealth. Instead they were purposefully kept from improving their quality of life, anchored to poor neighborhoods.

In *The Color of Law*, Richard Rothstein details how the FHA's underwriting manual provided clear steps to keep Black families out of areas of opportunity. In Detroit during World War II, for example, the FHA required that a developer construct a six-foot-high cement wall to separate a white development from a neighboring Black community, ensuring that no Black person could even step foot in it. Rothstein reminds us that while redlining became illegal in 1968, the effects of this federally sanctioned segregation are still evident today: "We have created a caste system in this country, with African Americans kept exploited and geographically separate by racially explicit government policies. Although most of these policies are now off the books, they have never been remedied and their effects endure."[2]

Falsely believing the stains of redlining disappeared when these policies were deemed illegal has allowed communities of color to remain structurally excluded from opportunities and wealth building by geographic boundaries. Redlining policies were seeds, planted and nurtured long enough for divisions to thrive even after these practices were deemed illegal. Through the years, the seeds were watered, encouraged by other racist policies—some that predated redlining, others that were created in its wake—like discriminatory mortgage lending, exclusionary zoning laws, racial covenants, biased GI Bill home loans, and urban renewal projects as well as by potent rhetoric that blamed struggling families for not working hard enough. At the same time, the system allowed white Americans to amass generations of wealth through homeownership and access to more resources under the falsehood that they simply worked harder.

The majority of these neighborhoods never rebounded from the ripple effects of discriminatory housing practices, and years later, the families that call them home still look the same. According to a 2018 report from the National Community Reinvestment Coalition, nearly 75 percent of redlined neighborhoods in the US are still low- to moderate-income,[3] and three-quarters of their residents identify as people of color.[4] The intention was to starve Black and other marginalized families of wealth and power by relegating them to desolate and deficient places, making it extremely difficult for them to flourish and even harder for them to escape. In his essay in *The Atlantic*, "The Case for Reparations," Ta-Nehisi Coates makes the agenda of keeping Black communities geographically separate and deprived very clear: "With segregation, with the isolation of the injured and the robbed, comes the concentration of disadvantage. An unsegregated America might see poverty, and all its effects, spread across the country with no particular bias toward skin color. Instead, the concentration of poverty has been paired with a concentration of melanin. The resulting conflagration has been devastating."[5]

There was little effort to hide this desired outcome. The Homeowners' Loan Corporation (HOLC) was a federal agency tasked with overseeing residential lending after the Great Depression. The agency created maps of 239 cities across the US and graded the neighborhoods from lowest (A) to highest (D) default risk for lenders, based on property values, economic class, employment status, transportation access, proximity to amenities, age and condition of housing, and, yes, racial makeup. HOLC's assessments are riddled with openly racist language, such as housing values decreasing because of a "strong colored infiltration" and a "detrimental change of ownership occupancy from white to colored."[6] The Federal Reserve Bank of St. Louis conducted a recent study tracking the number of Black Americans residing in HOLC-graded neighborhoods across the country between 1910 and 2010; results showed the largest concentrations of Black Americans were in the lowest-graded neighborhoods, with very few of them residing in neighborhoods where property values were either stable or increasing.[7] America's caste system was bolstered by an unapologetic geographic separation of families based on the color of their skin, a hierarchy that dictated every aspect of their lives.

Old HOLC maps labeled downtown Newport News, where my boyfriend and I lived during my freshman year of college, a D for "hazardous." In fact, in the 1930s, Newport News was one of the top ten US cities for the highest percentages of neighborhoods marked "hazardous" by HOLC—and almost 60 percent of the city fell in redlined zones.[8] When we lived there in 1999, our neighborhood evidenced this decades-long disinvestment: Dilapidated buildings with young children peeking out of the windows. Check-cashing stores instead of banks. Laundromats since most apartments didn't have washers or dryers. Hotels mostly used to sell drugs or meet prostitutes. Today, the poverty rate in Newport News is 14.7 percent,[9] higher than the state average (10.2 percent[10]) and the national average (12.5 percent[11]). Norfolk and Portsmouth, similarly densely redlined nearby cities, also continue to struggle with high poverty rates. Macon, Georgia, the city with the most "hazardous" areas in the 1930s—nearly 65 percent of its neighborhoods—has a poverty rate of 25 percent today.[12]

Low-income areas have some common traits, characterized mostly by what they *don't* have rather than what they do have. These neighborhoods are 4.5 times more likely to lack recreational facilities than high-income areas, and if they do have a recreational center, it's likely to be in poor condition.[13] A study conducted in five cities across California's San Diego County found that recreational centers in low-income neighborhoods were less likely to have high-quality and equipped gymnasiums, activity spaces, benches, and even trash cans. The same study also found that for every additional $10,000 in neighborhood income, the likelihood of having facilities in good condition jumps by 36 percent.[14] A 2021 report from the Trust for Public Land showed under-resourced neighborhoods have access to 42 percent less park space per person compared to their high-income counterparts.[15]

These communities are often called "book deserts," meaning very few retailers sell print resources, especially for young children, nearby. In 2016, Susan B. Neuman, a professor of childhood and literacy education at New York University, surveyed six metropolitan areas including Washington, DC's Ward 7 and 8 neighborhoods, the poorest sections of the District and the areas where most of the DC Scholars in our program live. She found that 830 children in these wards would have to share one book based on the dearth of book retailers in a twenty-one-mile radius.[16] When I lived in Newport News, I never saw a bookstore and didn't know where the library or community center was. And even if I had, getting to these places would have been tough, especially with a baby in tow.

Green space, play and fitness areas, and books are like water for human beings—we need these things to learn and grow. Without them, and other necessities like quality schools, banks, safe housing, and grocery stores, families are gridlocked in poverty. Discriminatory housing policies were more than restrictions on where people could live. They dictated who we could *be*. They created powerful, enduring geographical boundaries for where basic resources weren't allowed to exist for people of color. To access these resources, we would have to find a way *out*.

When we talk about families traversing poverty, we underestimate the importance of *place*, the power of finding our feet in spaces where opportunity lives. We miscalculate not only the advantages of being in those places but also the difficulty of getting to them for most people. American entrepreneur Ray Kroc, who expanded McDonald's from a small local chain to the world's most profitable restaurant franchise, once said, "The two most important requirements for major success are: first, being in the right place at the right time, and second, doing something about it." While Kroc worked his way up from selling milkshake machines to soda fountains nationwide, as a white man in the 1950s, he had access to places and opportunities that so many others didn't. He trained alongside Walt Disney in World War I, who became a lifelong professional friend. Decades later, in 1948, President Harry S. Truman signed Executive Order 9981 calling for the desegregation of the US armed forces. Until that point, a person of color would never have had the opportunity to build a close relationship with an entrepreneurial mastermind like Disney. Through McDonald's franchising, Kroc met businessman Harry J. Sonneborn, who helped him secure a $2.7 million loan to buy out the McDonald brothers in 1961 and gave him a key real estate strategy for the company. In 2008, then senator Barack Obama explained that even with the best business idea, throughout history, "Legalized discrimination—where blacks were prevented, often through violence, from owning property, or loans were not granted to African American business owners, or black homeowners could not access FHA mortgages, or blacks were excluded from unions, or the police force, or fire departments—meant that black families could not amass any meaningful wealth to bequeath to future generations."[17] This discrimination excluded Black and Brown people from rooms where handshakes over deals happened. Meanwhile, these rooms and relationships helped Kroc amass a net worth of $500 million by his death in 1984, and a personal estate worth more than $2.3 billion by 2002. Kroc was right: place is a major factor in success.

Place is determined by many things and, for many people, by forces that are out of our control. Lawful segregation, like redlining, has historically kept people of color from opportunity, while insidious, less obvious policies have physically restricted movements to access spaces that could accelerate their economic mobility. In other words, families with low income are not only kept from living in places by historic and present housing discrimination and segregation; they also lack reliable ways of *getting to them*.

For families in poverty, transportation is both an unworkable luxury and a major sacrifice. They are forced to spend a higher proportion of their income on transportation than wealthier families, and they're more likely to carpool, bike, or walk long distances to get to a doctor's office, grocery store, or bus stop.[18] A 2018 study of California's Maternal and Infant Health Assessment found that mothers in poverty "walked,"

"walked and took public transportation," or "rode a bike" more often than affluent mothers, and those walking or biking in unsafe neighborhoods were more likely to be mothers of color.[19]

Despite the welfare queen trope that depicts mothers of color as unmotivated and lazy, data shows that they actually work *harder* to get from one place to another. In other words, mothers of color have no choice but to be more motivated and extremely driven. During my freshman year of college, when my transportation insecurity was at its peak, I walked both the winding red brick paths on William & Mary's lush, green campus to get from one class to another *and* Jefferson Avenue's broken sidewalks in Newport News, pushing Nerissa in her stroller to wash loads of clothes at the laundromat or to buy milk at the 7-Eleven. In both cases, people made assumptions about who I was and what I was capable of, and I existed in these starkly different, dual realities—one vital to escaping the other.

When Generation Hope opened our New Orleans program in 2023 to support teen parents in college there, young parents and community groups cited reliable public transportation as a major challenge. On average, in New Orleans—where families of color are six times more likely to live in poverty than white families[20]—buses arrive on schedule only 73 percent of the time. It's even worse in other parts of the city, like New Orleans East, which has a large Black population.

For Alicia, one of our New Orleans Scholars, a young Black mother living in the Lower Garden District and raising her nineteen-month-old son, the unreliable Regional Transit Authority (RTA) makes what should be a forty-five-minute ride to her surgical technician classes at Delgado Community College nearly impossible. The RTA also causes her to miss doctor's appointments, so when she's sick, the emergency room has become the easiest place for her to access medical care. Alicia wants to create a better life for her son. She has goals and a strong work ethic, but like millions of parents with low income, especially young parents, she needs a way *to get there*.

Researchers at the University of Michigan have developed the first validated measure of transportation security, the Transportation Security Index, which offers insights into who experiences transportation challenges and how to craft solutions. The index found that nearly one-quarter of adults ages twenty-five and older in the United States experience transportation insecurity, meaning they are unable to move from place to place in a safe or timely manner. According to their research, more than half of the people living below the federal poverty line experience transportation insecurity, which is higher than the rate of food insecurity among people in poverty. Transportation insecurity is more common among Black adults (33 percent) and Hispanic adults (29 percent) than white adults (19 percent). Those most likely to experience transportation insecurity are residents of urban areas (39 percent), followed by those of suburban areas (22 percent) and those of rural areas (13 percent), and transportation insecurity rates are higher among people who don't own a car (42 percent) than car owners (18 percent).[21] Other research has shown that transportation insecurity is higher among women.[22]

Some argue that the country's disinvestment in public transit fuels transportation insecurity. The Inequality Project estimates that in recent decades the federal government has invested four times more in roadways than public transportation, like buses and subways.[23] This underinvestment contributes to malfunctioning buses and trains, a backlog of maintenance requests, and delayed public transit expansion projects, similar to the problems families are experiencing with the RTA in New Orleans. More than a thousand miles away, in the DC area, our students who rely on public transportation use the Metro, the nation's third-largest heavy rail system with six lines, 118 miles of track, and ninety-one stations.[24] In 2022, the average wait time for Metro trains in high-poverty neighborhoods in the District was twenty-one minutes while the average wait time in wealthier neighborhoods was just eleven minutes.[25] Back down south, in Dallas, Generation Hope's newest site, transportation similarly plagues families in poverty. The Dallas Area Rapid Transit (DART) trains arrive at stations every twenty minutes on average outside of peak hours, and out of their seventy-three non-express bus routes, only four arrive every fifteen minutes, with the rest operating every twenty, thirty, or sixty minutes.[26] Imagine the difficulty and stress of waiting that long with a baby on your hip, a shift at work you can't miss, and an evening class on the other side of the city taught by an unforgiving professor.

While building out roadways might seem like a solution to transportation insecurity, it overlooks the significant disparity between those who own cars in this country and those who don't. About 18 percent of the US population are carless, but the number is higher among certain groups.[27] According to the US Census Bureau, only 67 percent of Black households own vehicles, compared to nearly 82 percent of all households and 86 percent of white households. When looking at vehicle ownership by income level, the disparity becomes even more significant: only 61 percent of the lowest-income households own a vehicle compared to 90 percent of the highest-income households. The solution isn't all families purchasing cars. Car ownership is more expensive for families with low income. Gas, insurance, and maintenance eat up a larger share of their after-tax income than wealthier families. In 2022, the Bureau of Transportation Statistics reported that lower-income households spent 30 percent of their after-tax income on transportation while the highest-income households spent just 12 percent.[28] A deprioritized public transportation system makes mobility not only extremely difficult for families without cars but creates a heavier burden for families in poverty *with* cars.[29]

In the early 1990s, the vision for what we know today as ride-sharing, such as Uber and Lyft, began to emerge. These platforms capitalized on GPS technology, smartphones, and electronic payments to create a convenient system to connect passengers with drivers. In many ways, ride-sharing has expanded equity in transportation, providing an option for getting from point A to point B beyond having to own a car or live near a Metro stop. While taxis have been around for a long time, the industry has been unreliable for Black riders and those living in low-income neighborhoods. Research has found that taxi rides for Black passengers were 73 percent more likely to be canceled and took 52 percent longer to arrive.[30] The same research shows that this discrimination is less likely with ride-sharing platforms. But an Uber or Lyft ride to get to a doctor's appointment or a job interview isn't cheap. A one-way trip may cost forty-five dollars, or three hours of work if you're making fifteen dollars per hour. Researchers at George Washington University also found that passengers going to and from low-income and non-white neighborhoods may pay higher prices because of the algorithms of the ride-sharing apps.[31] Depending on the time of day, my freshman-year commute to drop my daughter off at her aunt's house and then to campus for class would have been about $100 one way or $200 round trip—a crippling cost.

The American dream isn't possible without a way to *get there*, and if college is a pathway to a better life, then it, too, is impossible without reliable transportation. Despite this, our policies and institutional supports cater to a very slim minority of students who live on campus rather than the vast majority—more than 85 percent—who rely on a car, public transportation, a bike, their own two feet, a carpool, or a ride-sharing service to get to class every day.[32] Commuting to college, crammed between multiple jobs and family responsibilities, is an expensive challenge for the 43 percent of undergraduate students with low income and for the nearly a quarter who are parents.[33] If a mother or father living paycheck to paycheck is contemplating a postsecondary credential, transportation becomes one of the top considerations, right up there with tuition costs and childcare expenses.

Transportation not only influences whether someone applies to and enrolls in college; it also determines whether they *stay in* college. In 2019, Karen, one of our Scholars in the DC area, was featured on *Good Morning America*. The television network paid for her train ride up to the studio in one of Manhattan's high-rise buildings, where I found her in the backstage maze with her young daughter, Gloria, bopping around on the couches. Through a shaky smile, Karen admitted how nervous she was, and I gave her the advice I give to students who are about to share their experiences: "You know your story better than anyone else." Just a few minutes later, she and Gloria were sitting on stage with the anchors, smiling brightly under the intense lights as Karen talked about being a mom in school. But in a seven-minute-and-forty-second segment, the audience misses what's hardest—the hidden, quiet, and most difficult moments. Like how tired Karen was because she took all of her classes either in the early morning or late at night so she could work during the day. Or how hard the drive to class at Northern Virginia Community College and then George Mason University was, whether she took the back roads or the major highways. Three years later, she wrote about the continued challenges on our blog, "As a commuting student, I was always calculating how long it was gonna take to get to campus and to class. I couldn't afford a parking pass, so I had to walk well over a mile to get to my classes. . . . I am not like other students. I don't live on campus. My parents cannot pay for my classes. Books and diapers are always on my mind. I don't want to turn things down at the last minute, but sometimes the last minute is all I have left."

Karen was "down to her last minute" at a community college and then at a university. The type of institution didn't matter. Commuting was always hard. In theory, public broad access institutions like community colleges, which admit at least 80 percent of their applicants, should be conveniently located and easier to get to than a university. Except about thirty-five million people, or 10 percent of the US population, live in higher education deserts, which according to a 2019 report by Nick Hillman, an associate professor of educational leadership and policy analysis at the University of Wisconsin-Madison, is defined as "a local area where there are either zero or only one public broad-access colleges nearby."[34] Thirty-five million people, many of them parents, have to travel farther to access educational opportunities—an extremely difficult task for those living in poverty.

Public transportation stops don't necessarily solve the problem. A 2021 study conducted by the Seldin/Haring-Smith Foundation found that only 57 percent of community college main campuses have a public transit stop within walking distance, yet 99 percent of community college students live off campus.[35] A car doesn't always solve every transportation challenge either. Even if a student owns or has access to a car, parking passes, as Karen pointed out, are often too expensive, forcing parents to park off campus and walk long distances to class. At a recent meeting with faculty and staff at Norfolk State University, one parenting student recalled how taxing the walk across campus was when she was pregnant with twins. The foundation also examined the proximity of public transit stops to the more than 16,400 Head Start centers across the United States. The analysis showed that 29 percent of the centers aren't near any public transit, or are more than five miles away, creating another transportation challenge for under-resourced parents who need childcare.[36]

Drawing from my own struggles with commuting to campus as a young mother, Generation Hope has invested in filling our students' transportation gaps since our inception. Our emergency fund provides $1,000 annually for our more than two hundred Scholars, and car repairs, gas cards, and Uber or Lyft rides are among the top requests. In 2023 alone, nearly a quarter of all emergency fund requests from our students were related to transportation. In most cases, without this relief, they wouldn't have been able to stay enrolled in college.

Long and difficult commutes are common threads woven through the journeys of the parents we work with and advocate for across the country. Providing for their children and changing their circumstances requires a daily, arduous, and complex quest to make it to a college classroom, far more challenging than what non-parenting and residential college students shoulder in their pursuit of a degree. It's a lonely and isolating mission, hard to fully understand and appreciate without living it. But there are so many of us who know the quiet dance of gathering up your things in the darkness and tiptoeing out of the house to get to an early work shift or a first class. We know the ache in your stomach when you have to put off paying the cell phone or electric bill to instead fill the gas tank. We know the need to quickly wipe away tears at the bus stop because you will be late again. We know the anxiety, the stress, the exclusions, and the constant drain on time and energy that takes away from studying for a class and spending time with your children. But this is all silent, quiet suffering in the midst of whispers of "lazy," "unmotivated," and "indifferent." We know all of this.

Unfortunately, these whispers ring louder than the stories of families with very little working so hard to get ahead, making it easier for policymakers and institutional leaders to dismiss transportation insecurity as an inconvenience rather than a significant hurdle for the millions of parents who can't live on campus but want to earn a degree or credential. Policies that support parents getting to colleges and universities, such as expanded public transportation, reliable transit systems, affordable vouchers or passes, and walkable communities with satellite campuses in low-income neighborhoods, are critical at the state and local level. Projects that seek to address rather than reinforce America's long history of utilizing infrastructure to segregate and oppress will be the most impactful. But success would have to be measured not in dollar signs for developers but in whether these projects shift power, access, and resources to communities long stripped of better connections to jobs, education, healthcare, safety, wellness, and other resources.

We are seeing increased awareness of the role that place and transportation play in an individual's ability to thrive and potential investments in removing geographic barriers to success. In 2022, US Department of Transportation secretary Pete Buttigieg announced a $1 billion plan to reconnect marginalized communities to economic opportunities via transportation infrastructure. At a press conference about the program in Birmingham, Alabama, a city deeply divided and still haunted by redlining, Secretary Buttigieg said, "Birmingham's a place that reminds us that there's always been a relationship between the physical ability to move about, and basic questions of fairness."[37] Two years later, Birmingham applied for funding under the Reconnecting Communities program to convert Fourth Avenue North from a one-way street to a two-way street and move traffic through the historic Black business district, including the Carver Theatre—one of few places that screened first-run films for Black people during the Jim Crow era—a neighborhood once divided and cut off by the construction of Interstate 65 in the 1960s.

In 2024, Representative Hank Johnson from the Atlanta area introduced a bill, Stronger Communities Through Better Transit Act, proposing $20 billion annually over four years in historic federal funding to help transit agencies expand frequency, reliability, hours, coverage, and service in low-income neighborhoods. The bill would disrupt a long history of federal funding that prioritizes the maintenance and construction of roads and highways over expanding public transit. When he introduced the bill, Representative Johnson said, "Transit in our communities is as essential as food on our tables, clothes on our backs and a roof over our heads." He and sixty cosponsors recognized that economic mobility in America is predicated on place and mobility, as essential as enough food to eat and a warm bed to sleep in.

Colleges and universities also play a role in clearing a path to campus for those who are kept farthest from their classrooms. To reach parents in under-resourced communities, institutions must enhance their supports for commuting students and couple them with supports for caregiving students. Gathering data on parenting status and transportation challenges before a student even steps on campus can help administrators understand the types of investments and tailored services they might need. Offering special sessions with childcare for commuting students during orientation to review transportation passes, vouchers, Uber or Lyft stipends, bike rentals, parking discounts, car repair programs, and other campus or community resources can help them get the answers to their questions before they even ask. College emergency funds should cover the transportation emergencies that can derail class attendance, such as a canceled bus route or a car repair, while also accounting for the additional transportation needs parents face, like getting their children to childcare.

Colleges should provide training for faculty and staff on transportation challenges unique to the surrounding community—and how they might impact students' ability to make it to their class—and resources they can offer to help students facing a transportation emergency. Professors should be encouraged to offer as much flexibility as possible in their courses, like online tutoring, extra help, group work, and reminders for assignments and tests knowing that most of their students will be juggling multiple priorities outside of the classroom. If parents in isolated and marginalized communities believed these resources and supports existed and were truly accessible, making it to campus each day might seem possible—and so might a college degree.

Creating the conditions that allow all families to prosper requires an examination of their starting point. In *Brave Enough*, Cheryl Strayed writes, "We don't reach the mountaintop from the mountaintop. We start at the bottom and climb up. Blood is involved."[38] Even when well-intentioned, we mistakenly focus on getting people to the destination—good pay, a certification, better housing. But for the millions of families surrounded by unpaved roads, overgrown yards, and boarded up storefronts, the destination, regardless of the actual distance, is incredibly far. Sometimes too far to even see. We forget how much blood is involved in getting to that mountaintop.

In the early days of Generation Hope I went into DC's public high schools to meet with students who were either parenting or expecting a baby to recruit them to our program. The schools were typically in the most impoverished parts of the city, mostly Black neighborhoods with a history of disinvestment so severe that at one time many of the homes lacked running water and electricity.[39] I drove through public housing and run-down row homes to get to the schools, where I often walked through metal detectors and showed the contents of my bag to school security guards. In a classroom, usually during their lunch periods, maybe seven or eight of us would sit around a table with pizza and chips and talk about parenting, their education, and what our program offered. This taught me early on one of the most important lessons in economic mobility work—the value of coming to families, being in their neighborhood, and sitting with them at their starting point. It helped me understand why so many of them looked back at me with distant gazes and critical eyes. Their starting point was intentionally kept far from higher education. They knew it, and now I could feel it.

We typically stay out of these spaces because it's easy to. Getting there requires us to travel outside of our normal commute, to drive a bit longer, to get off at an unfamiliar Metro stop. So we don't hear the stories or have a real sense of what is required to get to the mountaintop, and all the while, the silence remains deceptively peaceful. Change happens when we seek out and amplify those voices, meet families at their starting points, walk in the shoes of tired mothers and grandmothers, hear and appreciate the history of neighborhoods long forgotten. Ignoring the significance of place and the intentional barriers that prevent whole communities from moving freely in pursuit of a better life means we're destined to reinforce the very boundaries and exclusions that brought us to this point. America's systems intentionally kept non-white families in their place to limit their power and to rob them of their peace, and this violence is ever-present. It exists under the surface. It supersedes geography. It follows. It pursues.

In her book *The Warmth of Other Suns: The Epic Story of America's Great Migration*, Isabel Wilkerson shares an account of Jaqueline Joan Johnson, who migrated along with approximately six million other Black people from the South to other areas of the country from the 1910s through the 1970s. Johnson left her home in Charleston, South Carolina, for New York in 1971 hoping to find peace and prosperity there. On the surface, this pilgrimage from the South to the North for safety and stability was deceivingly sanguine, but Johnson understood how treacherous and violent it really was: "It occurred to me that no matter where I lived, geography could not save me."[40]

CHAPTER 7

FOOD AND THE ORDER OF THINGS

More than eight thousand years ago, a single salt crystal changed the world. Maybe the discovery happened while sitting by a lake or spring as the afternoon sun boiled the water down, leaving the translucent white cubes behind, or while accidentally unearthing ancient evaporated seabeds, but salt would determine the fate of civilizations, the outcome of wars, the profitability of trade routes, the exploration of new worlds, the victors of political conflicts, and the recipients of vast wealth. From the Shangxi province of China to Egypt to Romania, salt became one of the world's most valuable commodities—sustaining life and spilling blood to keep hold of power and control. In America, it incited war and built historic landmarks. Early colonists were forced to rely on salt imports from Britain because it was so scarce in the colonies, fueling taxation resentment and calls for revolution. The Erie Canal, a 363-mile waterway connecting the Hudson River to Lake Erie for salt transportation, took eight years to build, and thousands of workers, many of them poor Irish immigrants, died in the process.[1] All for *salt*. This "white gold" was so valuable that the English word *salary* comes from the Latin word *salarium*, which means "salt money" or "monthly allowance." In his book *Salt: A World History*, Mark Kurlansky reminds us, "Salt is so common, so easy to obtain, and so inexpensive that we have forgotten that from the beginning of civilization until about 100 years ago, salt was one of the most sought-after commodities in human history."

What made salt so valuable wasn't just its sharp, earthy taste. Salt draws moisture out of the cells of foods and bacteria through a process called osmosis, slowing bacterial and mold growth. It became one of the most effective ways to preserve food, essentially giving those who had it a reliable food supply. Salt was so valuable because of what it made possible.

There is no better argument for the power of food than a single briny rock accelerating human progress and development. To have food is to have time, ability, endurance, relief, energy. To be hungry is to be operating in a constant state of urgency, disadvantage, exhaustion, confinement. These polarities were clear and deemed advantageous well before the discovery of salt around 6000 BCE, and they continued to be leveraged throughout history. During slavery in America, plantation owners kept food rations dangerously low not only to maximize profits but to starve enslaved people of the strength and stamina to fight back or escape. For half a century, colonists overran Dakota Territory in the Minnesota Valley, forcing Native Americans onto small reservations along the Minnesota River, where corrupt federal Indian agents withheld food until they received illegal payments. From 1942 to 1964, the Bracero Program, a US government effort that brought millions of Mexican men to orchards, vineyards, and fields to temporarily work as farmhands, kept earnings so low they could barely feed themselves the food they harvested for others, all in the name of keeping costs down.

Both a requirement of and an impediment to economic mobility, food was—and still is—the currency of the American dream.

There seems to be a proverb for every situation we might be facing, every question we could be grappling with in life, from death to leadership to managing our finances. An African proverb gives us a lesson in our interconnectedness: "We have left our pot unwatched, and our food burns." Traditions and practices vary from tribe to tribe and region to region, but the value of collective responsibility is unmistakable in African culture. In Swahili, a Bantu language spoken in a stretch from Lamu Island, Kenya, to the southern border of Tanzania, it is described as *Ujima*. The idea is that we are all responsible for one another, that my success is reliant upon your success, that our negligence carries repercussions not just for the most vulnerable among us but for all of us, that bad things happen when we're not united. A Zulu proverb reflects the same sentiment, calling it *Ubuntu*: "I am a person through other people. My humanity is tied to yours." South African Anglican archbishop Desmond Tutu, who fought against apartheid, a policy that sanctioned racial segregation and discrimination against non-whites in his country, described Ubuntu as "the essence of being human—that a person is a person only through other persons, that my humanity is caught up in yours. I am fully me only if you are all you can be." In American culture, the absence of these values is unambiguous. We don't subscribe to the ideals of Ujima or Ubuntu. Instead, a person's suffering is of their own making and their own cross to bear. These beliefs have encouraged us to wander too far from the fire that warms our pot of food, abdicating our collective responsibility to ensure that no one goes hungry. As a consequence, at the very least, our food will burn, and at worst, the sparks will jump beyond the pot and spread like wildfire, consuming everything we hold dear.

People will starve. It's the unfortunate order of things. Some of us will go hungry. Children will subsist on very little, their bellies shrinking like raisins. Mothers will slowly push their plates to the middle of the dinner table again so others can eat. Fathers will drag themselves through the door empty and worn from their second job as long as the bills are paid. Still, they must work hard, show up, perform, excel. And this is all normal. Starvation is an inevitable, ugly reality of existing. We must accept that some of us will have enough, and some of us just won't.

These lessons begin at a very young age. We're conditioned to be disempowered spectators as a predetermined way of the world swirls around us, requiring that people suffer—sometimes die—over a daily bowl of rice, a ration of fruit, or a regular ham sandwich. Inevitable suffering is justified and reinforced through rhetoric and systems, but no matter how many times we see it or hear it, most of us feel a discomfort, a pang that tells us hunger isn't predetermined but allowed, even created. In her book *Untamed*, Glennon Doyle describes our uneasiness with the way things are "supposed to be": "[S]omething inside us rejects it. We know instinctively: This is not the intended order of things. This is not how things are meant to be. We know that there is a better, truer, wilder way. That better way is the unseen order inside us."

It was an unseen order that propelled me to start Generation Hope. It began crystallizing in May 2003 during my college graduation ceremony in William & Mary Hall, the same large arena I sat in four years before as a new mother and disorientated freshman. While I listened to our commencement speaker, Queen Noor of Jordan, impart her wisdom to all of the graduates from the podium on stage, my stomach looped itself around and around until it formed a tight knot of excitement and disbelief. I. Had. Actually. *Made it.*

I scanned the sea of people in the stands above, trying to find my family, mostly my little girl. Seeing her face—the same tiny nose and deep almond eyes I looked to for motivation on the hardest days over the past four years—would confirm it was real. And that's when it surfaced. While I searched for her, I felt the pang. A slight discomfort emerged. An uneasiness that originated from the center of my chest and would only grow in intensity as the months went by. At first, I was annoyed by it and annoyed with myself that I couldn't just enjoy the moment. I'd dreamed of this. I'd worked so hard to get here. Why couldn't I just savor and appreciate it? And then I was confused by the pang. Why would I feel *sadness*, of all things, on my graduation day? No, this was a happy, joyous time. A celebration. But as my eyes continued to dance from row to row, face to face, it occurred to me how rare my baby girl was in that audience. Among the crowd, shifting in their seats with excitement, she was likely the only three-year-old trying to prop herself up high enough to catch a glimpse of her mother graduating with a bachelor's degree somewhere down below. I was reminded that she and I were anomalies.

In 1998, I became pregnant along with about 12,537 other ten- to nineteen-year-olds in Virginia.[2] Statistically, only 5,015 of us would graduate from high school and less than 250 of us would earn a college degree before we turned thirty. That means 7,522 of us would have to find a way to provide for our children without a high school diploma, and 12,287 of us would have to feed, clothe, and shelter our families without a degree for at least another ten, fifteen, or twenty years.

I barely made it through college—not because I couldn't keep up academically. I did well in my classes, making the dean's list most semesters, but logistically, every day I walked a tightrope with my housing, transportation, childcare, and food supply hanging in the balance. I carried the stress around campus like a backpack full of bricks, but still I had to show up to my lectures on the shared characteristics of living organisms or Newton's first law of inertia and steady flight. Unsolvable calculations about how I would pay our bills each month crowded my thoughts, but I had to sit and listen to professors who seemed completely disconnected from my daily realities and take copious notes. My evenings were a blur of childcare pickups, dinners, baths, books, and bedtime, but I had to study until the early hours of the morning so I could do well on my tests and essays. Every day was fragile and impossible.

By the time we threw our black caps into the air marking the end of the ceremony, I fully understood the pang. I feared it, but I understood it. The way the world worked, Nerissa and I weren't supposed to be in William & Mary Hall for my graduation that day. We were supposed to be somewhere else, trying to find our way through the ugly, unfortunate order of things like the 12,287 other teen girls who saw two pink lines on their pregnancy tests the same year I did and who didn't have a college degree. That was the sadness. Nerissa and I were in the arena, and the others weren't. And I understood why it found me on a day full of happiness. It was calling me to create a new, better, and truer way.

Bringing five human beings into the world—two girls and three boys—means people often ask me for parenting advice. When they do, my first response is to ask *them* for parenting advice. My second response is to tell them that mothering at a young age with very little forced me to learn what children really need and gave me clarity on my mission. More than twenty years ago, when Nerissa was just an infant and I couldn't afford baby wipe warmers or a Diaper Genie, I started the practice of asking myself the same question every night before I went to sleep, a practice that continues now for her and her four siblings. *Today, did I do my best to ensure that all of my children were fed, safe, and knew they were loved?* If I can say yes to that question, then that day, I succeeded. Those are my three most important responsibilities as a mother, and at various points in my parenting journey, I've navigated differing degrees of difficulty and ease in ensuring the first two—never the last.

From the moment a child is born, they are hungry. Hungry for their mother's sweet milk, for the protection of someone's arms, and for the feeling of warm skin pressed against their own. At a very basic level, as parents, our job is to feed them in these ways as they grow. Because a child who consistently lacks food, safety, and love never fully grows into the person they're supposed to be. Their struggle to survive stunts their becoming, their full realization. But it's an impossible task to give something we don't have, and too many mothers and fathers have never reached their own full potential, never having been adequately fed, held, and loved themselves. They are stretched thin by systems and structures that protect the few and leave millions of families devoid of sustenance, security, and community while demanding that they work harder if they want more.

Being hungry for days or months necessitates a constant brokering between your brain and your body. Each morning your mind instructs you to do essential things like getting dressed for work, packing your toddler's backpack, or walking to the bus stop, but craving nutrients, your body fights back. Without the fuel it needs, your body starts to consume its own energy reserves—carbohydrates, fats, and then the protein in your tissue, causing a constant state of fatigue and fogginess. Even the most critical and seemingly basic tasks become formidable. So you strike deals between your brain and your body. *If I eat this bag of chips, will it tide me over until dinner time? How long can I make this box of cereal last for a family of four? Without breakfast, will I have enough energy to make it through my shift at work?* The war begins anew every day, and there are never winners. The battle wears on you, sometimes even changes you.

As a young mother in college, I was a seasoned negotiator. I often sat in my classes literally starving. Besides possibly observing that I'd lost a few pounds, the other students and my professors had no idea how little I was eating or that in the midst of my scarcity, I had another mouth to feed. Some days I subsisted on only a granola bar. It was cheap and filling, and I'd learned that if I ate it in the middle of the day, I could make it to bedtime without anything else. Those were the days when our cabinets were bare, and what little food I had went to Nerissa. Cheese slices, apple sauce, cereal, a box of Kraft macaroni and cheese.

I knew when everything was about to dry up. It was about the time of the month that my financial aid dollars and WIC ran out. On those mornings, I was thankful that I could send Nerissa off to the childcare center where they provided healthy snacks and a full lunch, and I would prepare for a long day of classes, where I'd sit hungry, fixated on the granola bar in the front pocket of my backpack. Occasionally my girlfriends would take Nerissa and me to the dining hall on campus with the extra points on their meal plans, and those days were like Christmas. We ate waffles drenched in maple syrup and sandwiches stuffed with so much meat you had to use two hands to eat them. That's when an unfamiliar peace would wash over me, knowing that for at least a little while, our bellies would be full.

For people who have access to it, food seems so easy to attain, so available—like air. We observe people functioning each day—working long hours, taking care of children, hopping on the bus—giving the impression that they must have what they need. It may not be a lot, but they're at least *surviving*. And once they work a little harder, they'll have more than enough. Food is everywhere, after all. At the corner store. In the hallway vending machine. Crowding the table during workplace potlucks. Like air.

Except food isn't everywhere. For eighteen million households in the US, it's hard to come by. These families teeter at the edge of an invisible cliff, fearing at any moment, the little bit that they have will run out, and everything will fall. Like I did back in college, these parents broker deals for their survival. They have found their granola bar—that thing that allows them to move through the day with virtually nothing in their stomachs. Like I did, they go hungry so their children can eat. And like I did, they fight the internal battle of food and survival every day, without anyone knowing.

Aside from the fact that both food and air are a human right, the two are very different. The quality of air differs from one place to the next, but air is essentially a simple mixture of mostly nitrogen and oxygen, and as soon as we're born, with our first raw, shaky cry, we're able to breathe it. Food on the other hand has to be grown, nurtured, found, gathered, prepared, and bought. It's not available to us as soon as we're born. It's not guaranteed. It is an entirely different thing. Food is complex, multifarious, and for too many, inaccessible.

What's often lost in conversations about hunger is one of the most critical components of solving it—food is much more than sustenance or fuel. Yes, we need food to get from one day to the next, but food is also identity, ritual, comfort, memories, *life*. Chef and humanitarian José Andrés says food brings us back to our humanity: "If you are lost, share a plate of food with a stranger . . . you will find who you are."[3] Native American activist, economist, and author Winona LaDuke sees food as a traceable line back to our ancestors: "Food for us comes from our relatives, whether they have wings or fins or roots. That is how we consider food. Food has a culture. It has a history. It has a story. It has relationships."[4] Chef, cookbook author, and television personality James Beard believed that food is perhaps the one thing that can bring us all together: "Food is our common ground, a universal experience."[5] Author and grief counselor Dr. Alan D. Wolfelt describes food as language: "Food is symbolic of love when words are inadequate."[6] Culinary historian Michael W. Twitty depicts Southern cuisine as a delicious history of race, politics, wealth, and enslavement in America: "The food is an archive, a keeper of secrets."[7] Food is different to different people, the same to all people, and different to each of us at different times.

Depriving people of food robs us of more than nutrients and fuel. It strips us of our humanness. Lifelines to our ancestors and to the world around us. Open doors to connection and to the spoken and unspoken ways of being in community. Contexts and deeper understandings of our intricate journeys and generational histories. Invitations to sit around a table and experience the sugary, golden warmth of being *loved*. Going without food is going without life, going without closeness, going without ourselves. Men who don't have enough to eat are more likely to physically abuse their partners, and women who are food insecure are more likely to experience this abuse.[8] Parents who are dealing with food scarcity are less likely to nurture their children and be involved in their development.[9] Constant hunger makes it more likely that an individual will commit crimes—even violent crimes.[10] People who don't know where their next meal is coming from have higher rates of loneliness and are more prone to suicidal ideation and suicide attempts.[11] Without having enough food, it's harder to get up every morning, to focus on a task, or even to dream of something bigger. In 1825, Parisian politician

Jean Anthelme Brillat-Savarin wrote, *Dis-moi ce que tu manges, je te dirai ce que tu es*, or "Tell me what you eat, and I will tell you what you are." Forty-seven million people in America are simply *empty*.

In May 1968, a CBS TV documentary called *Hunger in America* thrust the realities and faces of hunger into America's living rooms. At the time, most people thought hunger was a thing of the past, something that plagued other countries rather than their own communities, but the footage of small children suffering from malnutrition and related diseases filmed in Alabama's Black Belt, Virginia's rural horse country, San Antonio's Latino neighborhoods, and Arizona's Indian reservations told the story of approximately ten million hungry Americans. Before *Hunger in America*, their daily fight for sustenance was hidden, but the documentary made it difficult to ignore, prompting policies and initiatives to feed the food insecure. Hearing a story or reading a startling statistic about food scarcity might not be enough to move us, but the undeniable image of a small child with sunken eyes or heartbreaking footage of a grandfather with gaunt, hollow cheeks and wasting muscles can grip us.

More than fifty years later, Americans are more aware. In 2023, nearly 70 percent of likely voters wanted the government to do more to address food insecurity,[12] and in 2021, nearly 90 percent saw hunger as a serious problem worldwide.[13] But acknowledging a problem alone doesn't solve it. Hunger has not only endured; it has grown. According to the latest data from the US Department of Agriculture (USDA), the number of people dealing with food insecurity every day in the United States skyrocketed from thirty-four million in 2021 to a mind-boggling forty-four million in 2022.[14] The nonprofit organization Move For Hunger reports this as "the highest rate and number of food insecure individuals and children since 2014, and . . . the largest one-year increase in food insecurity since 2008."[15] Before COVID-19 broke out in 2020, the overall food insecurity rate was at a twenty-year low since it was first measured in the 1990s. Any progress that had been made was unraveled by the virus and its impacts. Those who were food insecure before the pandemic found themselves struggling even more, and the recovery to pre-pandemic levels has been slow.

One in six Americans, including thirteen million children (about twice the population of Arizona), don't have enough food to eat or lack access to healthy food.[16] No community in America is immune—100 percent of US counties and congressional districts have some food insecurity.[17] More than half (55 percent) of US households participate in one or more of the three major federal nutrition programs: SNAP, WIC, or the free and reduced school lunch program.[18] If you're thinking these parents just need to work more hours, here's a fact: more than half of all food-insecure households have adults working full-time[19] and households with adults working multiple jobs are 43 percent more likely to be food insecure than those working a single full-time job.[20] Hunger is acute for our most vulnerable. Seventeen percent of households with children can't provide them with enough food to eat.[21] Almost seven million older Americans have to choose between buying groceries or keeping their homes warm in the winter.[22] With more expenses and less income, single-parent families have higher rates of hunger. Households headed by single mothers are nearly twice as likely to face food insecurity than those headed by single fathers[23] and four times more likely than those headed by a married couple.[24]

The same groups of people who have been historically kept from opportunity and resources in America have also been historically deprived of food. This is no coincidence. The USDA reports that the average food insecurity rate among Black and Latino people is just below 23 percent and more than 21 percent, respectively, compared to the rate among white people of nearly 10 percent.[25] In DC, where my organization is headquartered, the Black food insecurity rate is 24 percent and the Latino food insecurity rate is 15 percent, compared to just 2 percent for white residents.[26] In 2022, 29 percent of Black children in the US lived in homes where there wasn't enough food to eat. That's about one in three Black children.[27]

Hunger is everywhere, but more people who are food insecure live in the South, where poverty is disproportionately concentrated and where racist policies were a cornerstone of the region's economic strategy. About 82 percent of counties with the highest rates of food insecurity are in the South, despite it being home to less than half of all US counties.[28] The farther south you travel from the Mason-Dixon Line, a boundary between Maryland and Pennsylvania that together with the Ohio River served as the divide between states that enslaved people and those that didn't, the more food insecurity you'll find. In the midst of the jagged mountains and winding rivers of Arkansas, 18.9 percent of households experience more severe rates of food insecurity—the highest in the nation—followed by Texas (16.9 percent) and Mississippi (16.2 percent).[29]

In *The Cooking Gene: A Journey Through African American Culinary History in the Old South*, Twitty makes the connection between racial oppression and access to food in America clear: "Food, racism, power, and justice are linked. What I'm trying to do is dismantle culinary nutritional imperialism and gastronomic white supremacy with one cup of zobo made from hibiscus, one bowl of millet salad with groundnuts and dark green vegetables, and one piece of injera at a time."[30]

We see the amalgamated story of food, racism, power, and justice playing out in Arkansas. By 1860, more than 110,000 enslaved people lived in the state, and one in five white citizens were enslavers.[31] Slavery and its acceleration of cotton production became the backbone of the Arkansas economy, generating at least $16 million annually and making the state the sixth-largest cotton producer in the US.[32] Well after the Civil War, the historic reliance on slave labor continued to feed economic disparities between Black and white residents. In 2006, the estimated median household income for white residents was $40,009, compared to $23,265 for Black residents. In 2007, 4.4 percent of white residents were unemployed compared to 11.4 percent of Black residents.[33] In a 2024 *Arkansas Advocate* interview, Arkansas Food Bank CEO Brian Burton said one out of three Black people in the state don't have enough food to eat. There was little confusion as to why. "It's not just something that happened in the last year; I think this is a result of years and decades of people who have been marginalized, obstacles they've had to transcend and limited access to opportunity."[34]

Peanut soups and gumbos, collard greens, cornbread, sweet potato pie, salt pork, black-eyed peas, puddings, barbecued chicken and beef. On any given holiday, you'll find many of these dishes, known as American soul food, on picnic and dining room tables, their origins rooted in survival. Soul food sustained Africans and Black people during slavery. A gumbo of Western and west-central African recipes and techniques,

Native American crops, and European foods, soul food emerged from the cheap provisions that enslavers rationed to enslaved people, such as sweet potatoes, cornmeal, and salted fish. With very little time of their own, they could then supplement their rations with what they were able to grow in their own gardens, like cowpeas and beans, and with animals that they hunted, like deer and turkey.

On President George Washington's Mount Vernon plantation in Virginia, just outside of DC, the daily rations for an enslaved adult was one quart of cornmeal and five to eight ounces of salted fish, forcing people on the plantation to go "without a mouthful for a day, and sometimes two days" according to Washington's overseer Davy Gray.[35] While the Great Depression, which began in 1929, marked the onset of widespread hunger in the US, at the height of America's slave industry in 1860, nearly four million enslaved people—roughly 13 percent of the US population—were forced to endure horrific emotional and physical traumas in addition to extreme malnourishment. The story of hunger in America is as old as the story of America.

When Italian explorer Christopher Columbus came to the Americas in 1492, the original inhabitants of what is now the United States numbered between ten million and fifteen million. Four hundred years later—with their land stolen; their people slaughtered, enslaved, infected with disease, raped, and kidnapped; their treaties broken; their wealth seized; and their food systems destroyed—Native Americans numbered fewer than three hundred thousand.[36] Today, the American Indian and Alaska Native population accounts for 1.3 percent of the US population; it has never fully recovered from the devastating effects of colonization. Twenty-eight US counties are majority Native American, and eighteen of them (64 percent) are considered high food insecurity counties. In some areas, hunger is even more glaring. A 2019 UC Berkeley study found that nearly all Native American households (92 percent) in northern California and southern Oregon tribal communities suffer from food insecurity.[37] While roughly one in seven Americans overall don't have enough food to eat, about one in four Native Americans struggle to feed themselves and their families.[38] Our nation's very first people are among our most hungry.

Hunger didn't begin with the Great Depression, and it didn't end with COVID-19. It doesn't exist independent of racism and injustice. Food is power, and when it is withheld, it becomes a tool of oppression. Hunger isn't the necessary order of things. Since the founding of America, it is a thing that has been used to *create order*: slavery, genocide, marginalization. Hunger is alleviated by casserole ministries, canned food drives, and food banks, but it is only solved by widespread policy changes and structural shifts that uproot long-standing depravities and create a new normal that benefits everyone. For families to move out of poverty, we have to speak these truths, see our humanity as being bound up together, and stay close to the simmering pot that feeds us all.

In 2022, as most of the world was trying to leave the pandemic and its indisputable disparities behind, the *Washington Post* published an article entitled "Fathers or Students: Black Men in College Often Face a Choice," featuring one of our graduates, Joseph.[39] His journey raising his daughter, Jakayla, while attending the University of the District of Columbia Community College and then Howard University illustrated a larger problem across higher education that predated COVID-19 and that would outlast it: too many Black fathers are experiencing increased rates of housing and food insecurity without campus and community supports. Consequently, they're dropping out of school at higher rates than any other student-parent group.

Faced with a choice to either provide for their families or pursue their education, and without structures in place to ensure they can do both, 72 percent of Black fathers stop attending college and continue a familiar cycle of low-wage jobs, hungry mouths to feed, and not enough education to climb higher. Over the years, my team worked with Joseph, connecting him to resources, encouraging him, and surrounding him with a community that helped him earn his degree. We felt all of his exhilarating highs and dark lows, together. The graduation photos show a proud father wearing a royal blue cap and gown with a bright yellow, red, blue, and green kente-patterned stole draped around his neck while he embraced his daughter. But in reflecting on his journey, he told the reporter, "There were moments I felt like I failed her."

Black fathers face the impossible choice of feeding their families now or continuing their education in pursuit of higher pay later. This doesn't happen because food is scarce or production is slow, but because America has prioritized profit and wealth over people. Like so many hurdles families face when working toward a more stable future, hunger is just another manifestation of systemic failures. These include policies that keep wages low, allow underemployment or unemployment, weaken the safety net, exclude access to affordable quality healthcare, limit economic opportunities for entire communities through disinvestment, hinder educational attainment, suppress political engagement, invest in mass incarceration and criminalization, neglect housing insecurity, and continue or ignore discrimination based on race, gender, and disability.

The result is a hunger crisis that is unrivaled by any other industrialized nation.[40] Among all seven of the world's advanced economies including Canada, France, Germany, Italy, Japan, and the United Kingdom, the US has the highest proportion of its residents struggling to afford food (26 percent).[41] Our policy choices keep people hungry and our individualistic ideals—the opposite of Ujima and Ubuntu—absolve us of our responsibility to each other, especially to those in need. Nelson Mandela, friend and ally of Desmond Tutu, once said: "Like slavery and apartheid, poverty is not natural. It is man-made, and it can be overcome and eradicated by the action of human beings."[42] America created poverty and therefore created our hunger crisis, and there is no one else to fix it but us.

The choice to eat or learn carries lasting impacts not only for each individual and their family, but also for the possibility of reversing America's food insecurity. The number of hours a parent works doesn't necessarily determine if they will be able to bring more food into their homes, but it turns out that their education level does. According to a 2009 USDA study, food insecurity was ten times more likely in households in which none of the adults had completed high school (22 percent) than in households with an adult who had earned a four-year college degree (2.3 percent). In fact, only 10 percent of households with food-insecure children had an adult living there with a four-year college degree.[43] When a parent is forced to stop out of college because they need to feed their children, that actually increases the likelihood that their family will continue to grapple with food insecurity. If we want to eradicate hunger in America, we should include high school and postsecondary completion as key strategies in the fight. Bold policies should address educational disparities and the major conundrum that comes with them: education level determines access to food, but access to food also determines education level, especially for parents.

For the first time in its thirty-six-year history, in 2023, the National Postsecondary Student Aid Study (NPSAS), administered by the National Center for Education Statistics (NCES) at the US Department of Education, released data on the food insecurity of college students. In its study of 17.1 million undergraduates at Title IV–eligible institutions (colleges that offer federal student aid) at any time between July 1, 2019, and June 30, 2020, 23 percent of them—about four million—were food insecure, or had low or very low food security in the last thirty days.[44]

The data conflicts with the image of carefree, wealthy college students crowding most campuses and instead reflects the reality: the majority of college students today are balancing school with work and other family responsibilities, and a significant number of them don't have enough food to eat. While food insecurity is higher at community colleges (23.4 percent), it also plagues students at four-year nonprofit public schools (20.9 percent) and four-year nonprofit private schools (18.8 percent). Institutions that serve more students of color also have higher rates of food insecurity. Nearly two in five undergraduate students at HBCUs and more than one in three students at tribal colleges and universities report food insecurity.[45] The inequities on college campuses mirror the inequities across the country: Black students report the highest levels of need, with more than a third (34 percent) indicating food insecurity.

Parenting while in college intensifies this need. Twenty-three percent of all college students lack access to food, but in 2020, the Hope Center at Temple University released a study of twenty-three thousand students with children that found 53 percent were food insecure in the prior thirty days—and this data was from 2019, *before* the pandemic.[46]

Parents in college are experiencing food insecurity at more than double the rate of all college students, and rates climb even higher for certain groups of parents. The same study found that 70 percent of Indigenous parenting students at community colleges experience food insecurity compared to white student parents (51 percent), Black student mothers (66 percent), and white student fathers (41 percent). In 2023, Generation Hope found that 33 percent of our New Orleans Scholars and 26 percent of our DC-area Scholars were food insecure while raising young children, working, and going to college—most of them Black and Latina mothers. The increased costs of being both a parent and college student coupled with the discrimination that has long withheld food from communities of color means less money for Black, Latino, and Indigenous parents to pay for groceries—and less energy and capacity to make it to the graduation stage.

Students struggling with hunger are more likely to report lower GPAs,[47] poor sleep, higher levels of stress, eating disorders,[48] and missing class.[49] While in class, they operate on little fuel, making it difficult to concentrate, impacting their performance on tests, ability to engage in discussions, and participation in group work and projects. They're also about three and a half times more likely to consider dropping out of school than those who aren't worried about where their next meal is coming from.[50] On campus, professors and peers might interpret these struggles as evidence that a student doesn't care about their education—compounded by negative stereotypes about Black, Indigenous, and Latino students, gender biases, poverty shaming, and the stigma of being a parent in educational spaces. Instead of seeing someone who needs help, people often see someone who doesn't *deserve* help. Unsurprisingly, food insecure college students are 42 percent less likely to graduate[51] and have lower odds of earning a bachelor's degree or a graduate or professional degree.[52]

Three years after he earned his degree from Howard University, Joseph joined Generation Hope's board of directors, reflecting our commitment to including those we serve in helping to lead the organization. During a strategic planning retreat in 2023, we all sat in a hotel conference room, tables arranged in a U-shape, as we deliberated three possible growth scenarios for the organization. One scenario involved no growth. The organization would maintain the status quo. Another scenario would grow our direct services to a fourth city, where we would serve more teen parents in college while also bolstering our systems-change efforts. The last scenario would grow our policy work and our partnerships with colleges, but it would also invest more in the basic needs of our Scholars.

Board members shared their perspectives, weighing the financial and strategic ramifications of each option. Finally, Joseph raised his hand and offered what was missing in the conversation. Joseph, a father who had faced the hard, impossible choices and had graduated against all odds, reminded us of the urgency in our Scholars' days. He reminded us of how it feels to not know if you'll be able to feed your family tomorrow or if the childcare center will give you another extension to pay your child's tuition. We unanimously chose the scenario that called for a deeper exploration of supporting the basic needs of our students.

The hunger crisis won't be solved in hotel conference rooms or on the top floors of office buildings unless we're inviting the right people into those spaces or we meet them where they are, which is far from retreat centers and high-rises. The right people don't necessarily have fancy titles or a string of degrees behind their names. In fact, lack of food access has made those things impossible for most of them. No, the right people include those who have waged the daily war of hunger and survival. Those who have had to find their granola bar. Those who have looked into their children's eyes for strength and motivation, unsure of what tomorrow would bring. And once they're around the table, we must listen, because they have lived the things others have only theorized. We must listen to their uncomfortable truths, disruptive approaches, and unpopular solutions without interrupting with excuses about the impossibility of their ideas—not enough money, time, buy-in, or infrastructure. That's just rhetoric that justifies and normalizes hunger and oppression. We have to be open and creative and hopeful.

Before 1969, the idea that someone would walk on the moon was absurd, but once Neil Armstrong and Buzz Aldrin took those first historic steps on its rugged, dusty surface, it became real and possible. Buzz Aldrin once said, "If we can conquer space, we can conquer childhood hunger." Eradicating hunger is only absurd because we lack the willingness, innovation, investment, and courage to make it possible.

I wish the solution was as simple as giving people more food. That's a critical piece, but it lacks an understanding that hunger is a symptom of the bigger poverty problem in America—a brittle branch on a somber tree. While food banks and soup kitchens play a vital role and need more support, eradicating hunger will require a reckoning with the tree's deep, gnarled, ugly roots of greed and fear, and an examination of its other branches—low wages, underemployment and unemployment, lack of transportation, housing insecurity, and educational disparities. The fight against hunger happens in unexpected places. Yes, in the cafeterias at senior centers and in the rich soil of community gardens, but also in the echoing halls of Congress, championing legislation that makes it possible for families to pay their rent or mortgage, medical bills, tuition, and car repairs. These policies will help them afford groceries not just today but far in the future.

The Child Tax Credit (CTC), enacted in 1997 to give millions of families financial relief, has been shown to be one of the most effective tools for reducing child poverty. During the pandemic, the American Rescue Plan made significant expansions to the CTC, ensuring monthly rather than yearly funds for every family who needed them, with full benefits extended to about twenty-seven million children, including children of color, who would have previously received only partial funds or none at all.

The results were far-reaching. Sixty-one million children received the expanded CTC, cutting child poverty nearly in half, to a record low of 5.2 percent[53] and helping to reduce food insecurity by 26 percent in eligible households.[54] In 2022, when the pandemic relief expired, the child poverty rate more than doubled to 12.4 percent.[55] In August 2024, the Senate voted against a bill that would have expanded the CTC again. Senator Mike Crapo, a Republican from Idaho and ranking member of the Senate Finance Committee, said, "The bill does get a lot of things right. However, the critical flaw with the bill is that it fails to provide meaningful tax relief to working families and instead goes too far toward the Democrats' goal of turning the child tax credit into a subsidy untethered to work."[56] While legislators go back and forth, fueling the welfare queen trope that families in poverty don't want to work, people go hungry.

Policies that specifically target hunger should address how fragmented and limited supplemental food programs like WIC and SNAP are. With cumbersome application processes, unrealistic eligibility thresholds, benefits that don't cover the real costs of healthy food, limited options in grocery stores, and disconnected agencies, these programs, while cost effective and impactful, need to be strengthened and expanded to meet the true need.

SNAP is a critical anti-poverty and anti-hunger program, but even after the 25 percent increase in benefits after a reevaluation by the Thrifty Food Plan at the USDA in 2021, it provides an average of just $1.40 per person per meal each day.[57] WIC is a vital source of nutrition and well-being for nearly half of all babies in America as well as millions of children up to age five and their mothers, but it only reaches 51 percent of mothers who are eligible.[58] Instead of weakening these programs, we should be infusing them with funding and infrastructure to ensure that no one goes hungry.

The stigma of food insecurity also discourages individuals from accessing and utilizing benefits. Disapproving looks from people in the grocery store and in administrative offices can dissuade even the hungriest individual from stepping up to the cash register. Politicians often leverage this shaming and the public's nescience about what causes hunger to underfund or gut these programs. Though more than 80 percent of SNAP households include seniors, people with disabilities, and children,[59] and though WIC serves millions of pregnant and postpartum women with low income, infants, and young children at nutritional risk, these programs, while proven to be effective, are constantly under attack. In his fiscal year 2021 budget, President Donald Trump tried to revoke SNAP eligibility for approximately seven hundred thousand unemployed people, proposing more than $180 billion in cuts, reducing the program by nearly 30 percent over ten years. It wasn't an original idea. He was continuing a long-standing attempt by conservatives to weaken America's safety net programs to offset tax cuts to the wealthy. Solving hunger will require prioritizing SNAP and WIC over making the rich richer.

I have two grocery stores within a five-minute drive from my house—a large supermarket and a small, local organic store. Caught up in our daily routines, it's easy to assume this is the case for everyone, but for too many people, *finding* nutritious food is as challenging as affording it. Food deserts are areas where residents have limited access to healthy foods, especially fresh fruits and vegetables. It's not just about the lack of grocery stores and restaurants in these areas. It's also about the intentional placement and abundance of convenience stores and fast-food restaurants that follow patterns of redlining and historic segregation in these places, turning them into "food swamps." Nearly nineteen million people are estimated to have limited access to a supermarket,[60] with Black neighborhoods having the least access.[61] In 2011, at the Mayor's Summit on Food Deserts in Chicago, First Lady Michelle Obama told attendees, "It's not that people don't know or don't want to do the right thing; they just have to have access to the foods that they know will make their families healthier."[62]

We need policies that incentivize the strategic placement of supermarkets and local grocers in low-income communities and policies that establish alternative and convenient places for people to access food, whether at schools, nonprofits, businesses, local agencies, or places of worship, with the voices of community members leading the way. To ensure those who are most food insecure have plenty of food options close to where they live, legislators should encourage more local grocery stores to accept WIC and SNAP as opposed to forcing families with transportation challenges to travel to large chain stores that may be thirty minutes away or more. And just like well-resourced families can easily place orders online for food via Instacart, families with low income should be able to use SNAP and WIC to buy groceries online. Right now, one in six Americans rely on food banks, food pantries, and other meal distribution efforts, but these programs have been crippled by inflation and decreased government and public support after the pandemic, forcing them to buy less food and reduce services. We need more investments in these organizations if we want them to be effective.

If education is a long-term hunger solution, more people with low income, particularly mothers and fathers, should be able to pursue it. The welfare queen trope has effectively stifled legislation that would make significant investments in educating people in poverty while upholding and enacting policies that prioritize the low-wage jobs that keep them hungry. This racist mistruth is inconspicuously curled around the deep roots of the dying tree, feeding hunger and its sister branches. To kill it, we need policies that produce the opposite effect—policies that decrease tuition costs, make childcare less expensive, provide reliable and affordable transportation, include hours spent in a classroom as work requirements to access benefits, and create financial relief so learning is a right for all, not a luxury afforded to the few.

Colleges play a vital role in helping to remove the food barrier to earning a postsecondary credential. More than eight hundred US college campuses have food pantries, but they miss the mark if students, especially those who are most food insecure, don't know about them or are unaware of how they work. Campus food banks should be open during times when parents can access them, have few barriers to participation, and offer robust outreach strategies that recognize how limited student-parent time is. Campus and community organizations must recognize that students with children have more mouths to feed so they'll need more food than non-parenting students as well as nutritious kid-friendly options. During the 2022 nationwide infant formula crisis, for example, most campus food pantries didn't have infant formula on their shelves, which left parenting students scrambling to feed their babies.

Knowing that students who lack access to food are faced with stigma off campus as they try to secure food for themselves and their families, institutions can create stigma-free campus environments when it comes to parenting and hunger. From ensuring all faculty and staff have quick access to an up-to-date resource list for students battling food insecurity to educating the entire campus community about the root causes of hunger and poverty in America, schools can create a new normal.

There are famous black-and-white photos of harrowing marches through the streets and gripping speeches before seas of people, but I imagine the most pivotal moments of the civil rights movement took place in small offices, living rooms, cars traveling late at night, jail cells, and, yes, dining room tables. A modest kitchen in Montgomery, Alabama, that belonged to a Black woman named Georgia Gilmore was a little-known mainstay in the fight. A midwife by profession who lived just a few blocks from Dr. King, Gilmore opened her home—serving pork chops, stuffed bell peppers, chitlins with slaw and cut-up hog maw, pans of bubbling macaroni and cheese, and batches of fried chicken—to Dr. King and others in the fight for justice. The two formed a friendship undergirded by a shared discontent with America's treatment of Black people and a love for food as a balm for even the most wounded souls. After she lost her job as a cafeteria cook for testifying in court in defense of the 1955 Montgomery bus boycott, Gilmore took Dr. King's advice and turned her home into a backdoor restaurant, going into business for herself.

Word spread quickly about Gilmore's delicious food, so much so that people were willing to wait in line for it, and as soon as a table would empty, the next party would sit down. Dr. King often brought guests to dine, including President Lyndon B. Johnson and Senator Robert F. Kennedy. But Gilmore knew that food holds power, and she used her talents to feed more than just people. She fed the *movement*. Her house served as a surreptitious meeting place for Dr. King and other leaders, and she formed the Club from Nowhere, a group of women who sold pies and cakes at beauty shops, using the proceeds to provide alternate forms of transportation during the 381-day bus boycott. The club paid for church station wagons, insurance, gasoline, and car repairs in order to help transport people around Montgomery. Their customers included white people who opposed the boycott but were unknowingly helping to fund it.

Just as food is more than sustenance, Gilmore was more than a cook. She was an activist, and even though she was struggling to make a living and to care for her family like everyone else, her food was her superpower. In a July 2005 NPR story "The Kitchen of a Civil Rights Hero," a man said of her: "Well, I'd say Georgia Theresa Gilmore was one of the unsung heroines of the civil rights movement. You know, Martin Luther King often talked about the ground crew. She was not really recognized for who she was. But had it not been for people like Georgia Gilmore, Martin Luther King Jr. wouldn't have been who he was."[63]

King and Gilmore were both haunted by the uneasiness. The unseen order of things hummed, telling them that the torment and suffering of fifteen million Black Americans wasn't normal or necessary or right. It was undeniably inhumane. The pang called them to create a new, better way that would benefit Black people and, at the same time, uplift everyone. Our world is better today because while they feared its uncertainty, they answered it, each in their own way. Dr. King recognized selfless, unconditional love as the most powerful force against hate and oppression. Gilmore recognized food as the great unifier and a delectable enchantment to be leveraged for the greater good. They needed each other. The world needed both of them. Our fate was bound up together in theirs.

Gilmore's fearlessness reminds us that each of us has a superpower. The question is whether we'll use it to normalize suffering or to expose inhumanity. Like a single grain of salt, each of us can transform the world in historic ways that are uniquely ours. It won't come without risk or fear or consequences, but our actions could make it possible for future generations to grow up in a country that looks completely different from this one—a place of true prosperity where no one suffers needlessly and where we dance together around a plentiful, warm pot that feeds us all.

People will be nourished. It's the order of things. No one will go hungry. Children will have what they need to grow, their bellies full. Mothers will eat with the people they love around the table. Fathers will come home in time to cook dinner, the sounds of their children's giggles echoing from the backyard. And this is all normal. Because abundance is an inevitable, beautiful reality of believing in our collective humanity. All of us will have enough, and no one won't.

CHAPTER 8

HOUSING AND BEGINNINGS

There is sadness when a building falls. After the blows of the excavators, bulldozers, and cranes, its metal bones quiver, its wooden boards splinter, no longer able to hold its own weight. It leans and groans, trying to find the right place to land. Its recognizable parts—doors, windows, bath tubs, balconies—now look foreign and misplaced as they shift and stretch. The dust bellows with each fold, and then it disappears in a roaring wave of concrete, glass, and metal.

No matter the reason for the demise of a building, its demolition reminds us that at its beginnings, someone believed in it and took great care to design and construct it. They discussed every detail and made sure each measurement was just right. If it was a home, someone once walked through its door with excitement about all that could be, and over the years, birthdays, holidays, and other milestones were celebrated within its walls. When a building dies, each of these things dies with it, leaving only memories.

In 2007, the last building in Chicago's Robert Taylor Homes, once the largest US public housing project, came crashing down. For more than forty years, it stood as one of twenty-eight sixteen-story, densely packed, high-rise towers along a two-mile stretch in the historic Black Bronzeville neighborhood of Chicago's South Side. At one point, twenty-seven thousand residents, all living at or below the poverty line, resided in its more than four thousand units. Named after Robert Rochon Taylor—a Black architect and activist who became the first Black chairman of the Chicago Housing Authority (CHA) in 1942—the housing project began construction in 1959, despite protests from the *Chicago Defender* and the Welfare Council of Metropolitan Chicago. It was completed in 1963.

Taylor Homes was the result of a federal government effort after World War II to increase public housing and eliminate slum neighborhoods—areas with substandard and inadequate housing—through an effort called urban renewal. When he signed the Housing Act of 1949, which officially launched this initiative, President Harry S. Truman said of the legislation: "This far-reaching measure is of great significance to the welfare of the American people. It opens up the prospect of decent homes in wholesome surroundings for low-income families now living in the squalor of the slums. It equips the Federal Government, for the first time, with effective means for aiding cities in the vital task of clearing slums and rebuilding blighted areas."

But by nearly every measure, Taylor Homes was a failure. First, its location thwarted any possibility of "wholesome surroundings." The buildings towered over the Black Belt, a thirty-block area along State Street where the majority of Black Chicagoans lived in dilapidated, crowded housing. They had been funneled to this area for years. In response to roughly sixty thousand Black people migrating to Chicago from the South from 1940 to 1944 to find jobs, white residents created restrictive covenants, or legal agreements that prevented building owners from renting or selling to Black people. With nowhere else to go, families had to settle in the Black Belt. Landlords capitalized on their situation, crowding multiple families into one apartment and sectioning it into tiny units called kitchenettes while charging steep rents. As opposed to having their own bathrooms, residents shared a hallway bathroom, and during Chicago's cold winters, they were forced to rely on kerosene lamps and makeshift stoves to stay warm because the buildings lacked proper heating. The lamps and stoves often overheated and set their homes ablaze. One year, approximately 751 fires erupted in the Black Belt, many of them claiming the lives of the residents.

Starved of resources, the neighborhood was plagued by unemployment, poverty, and crime. In the planning phases of Taylor Homes, Robert Rochon Taylor knew how important it would be to locate public housing elsewhere, seeing it as a powerful tool for integration and new opportunities for Black Chicagoans. When the Chicago City Council disagreed, insisting public housing projects be placed in all-Black neighborhoods, he resigned. Ultimately, the strategic placement of Taylor Homes and other housing projects would only preserve Chicago's racial segregation and worsen the conditions for Black people. Taylor died in 1957 before construction on Taylor Homes was completed. In 1959, the *Chicago Defender* wrote, "Were Taylor alive today, he would strenuously disavow the association of his name with a Jim-Crow housing project."[1]

The next issue was that Taylor Homes was chronically underfunded from the start. Despite President Truman's promises, the towers offered families anything but "decent homes." They would soon mirror the struggling Black Belt neighborhood that surrounded them. The largest public housing project in the nation was a massive undertaking, not only in its construction but in its maintenance. The CHA lacked both the funding and the capacity to properly manage the housing project, and as a result, it soon fell into disrepair. Although it was originally intended to house eleven thousand residents, the population surged to more than double that number—many of them children—straining the towers and overwhelming CHA staff.

Engineering problems surfaced not long after completion, including malfunctioning elevators, failed heating systems, leaking pipes, and faulty electricity meters. Over the years, budget cuts further eroded any hope residents had of thriving, leaving unit repairs neglected and drastically reducing or eliminating wraparound services like after-school programs, free meal distribution, early childhood education, healthcare access, and community events. While there were many success stories, the conditions inside and outside Taylor Homes often undermined residents' efforts to succeed in school, secure good-paying jobs or promotions, maintain regular employment, and stay healthy.

One of the ultimate failures of Taylor Homes is one shared by so many public housing projects, whether the neighboring Cabrini Green Homes on the North Side of Chicago or Pruitt-Igoe in St. Louis, Missouri, or Magnolia Projects in New Orleans. Shelter is vital to every human being's basic survival, but it is not a magic wand that cures all ills and removes all barriers to prosperity, especially when that shelter is located in starved communities and perpetuates racial segregation and discrimination. Chicago's Black Belt public schools were severely underfunded and overcrowded. In 1957, the average white elementary school had fewer than seven hundred students, while the average Black school had nearly double that number.[2] Taylor Homes could not solve for under-resourced schools.

Black people were also still excluded from industries with higher wages and from many labor unions that could have helped negotiate better pay. In 1963, the unemployment rate for white Chicago residents was 2 percent compared to 6 or 7 percent for Black residents. In 1965, a non-white worker with a high school education was as likely to be employed as a white worker who hadn't even completed eighth grade.[3] These inequities restricted Black families in nearly every way, and almost twenty years after Taylor Homes first opened its doors, the neighborhood had become the poorest urban area in the United States.[4]

Families dealt with substandard living conditions. They were also cut off from real opportunities, basic safety and security, critical resources, and essential information that make it possible to move out of poverty. In her play, *A Raisin in the Sun*, which draws from her experiences growing up in Chicago's segregated South Side, playwright and activist Lorraine Hansberry illustrates this painful disenfranchisement when the character Lena Younger, referred to as Mama, says, "Seem like God didn't see fit to give the Black man nothing but dreams—but He did give us children to make them dreams seem worthwhile." Taylor Homes left too many residents with only dreams of a better life rather than a viable pathway to one.

There is a black-and-white photo of a gaping hole in the side of one of the Taylor Homes towers as it was being demolished that I imagine is hard for many former residents to see. In fact, two out of three residents didn't want the complex to be razed.[5] Taylor Homes was more than just a sprawling series of imposing, concrete edifices, casting their shadows over the city. Despite decaying conditions and the high rates of crime, poverty, and drugs, it was also a place of promise, relief, rebirth, family, and community. It was summer barbecues on the playground while a deejay spun rap and R & B songs for everyone to sing along to. It was gang members providing lunches or books for kids, and teenagers helping elderly residents carry their groceries upstairs. It was a neighbor two doors down who could watch your children while you went to work. It was a network that felt like family, even without blood relations.

In a *South Side Weekly* interview, former resident Christine Gayles describes her affinity for Taylor Homes: "Because, for me, it's my home and it's who I am. It's how I've come to be. The things and lessons that I've learned and witnessed and saw in the Robert Taylor Homes have had a lasting impact on my life, so it's like my legacy."[6] Gayles, whose mother and grandparents lived in Taylor Homes and other CHA buildings, later became a Chicago Public Schools teacher. She was just fifteen years old when she watched her building topple down.

The story of Taylor Homes is emblematic of our country's continuous progress toward—and failure to live up to—our ideals. It's a tale of bad and good intentions, racist legacies and enduring hope, selfish motivations and unity in adversity, all tangled together in the desperate fight for the soul of our country. It's a testament to the human spirit, the power of community, and the political machine with the ability to rip it all apart. Housing is fundamental to economic mobility, yet it can also be used to keep people from ever experiencing economic mobility. The day the last empty tower collapsed, the city could hear both a resounding sigh of relief and an agonizing cry of despair as it disappeared in all of its chaotic, beautiful glory.

There weren't many constants when I was pregnant with Nerissa. Uncertainty was the one thing I came to expect each morning, uncertainty about whether her father would be lying beside me or if he would be coming home at all, uncertainty about whether I'd have enough food to eat, uncertainty about whether I'd ever make it to college, uncertainty about my ability to carry the baby to term. Another worry woven through those forty-one weeks was whether we'd have a home to bring her to when we left the hospital. We'd spent most of my pregnancy sleeping in my boyfriend's car, on people's couches and floors, and in a Motel 6, and I couldn't imagine bringing a newborn baby to any of those places. I didn't need much—a tiny apartment with a bed and a stove to cook a meal would do. It just needed to be a place of our own. A home.

A couple months before I gave birth, we moved into a small one-bedroom apartment in St. James Terrace, a complex of red brick apartments on the James River in Newport News, Virginia. The apartments were connected to my boyfriend's new employment at the Newport News Shipyard. They were built in the 1940s, along with other complexes after the city's population soared by 77 percent, making it the second-fastest growing community in the nation.[7] By the time we arrived in 1999, the area, like much of downtown, had suffered from disinvestment, overshadowed by the shipyard's towering cranes, docks, piers, and massive ships. We furnished the apartment with a few things from a nearby thrift store, including Nerissa's crib, and tried to make it a home. Soon after, I slowly hobbled through its door, holding an eight pound, nine ounce, curly-headed baby girl in my arms, happy that I could at least give her this.

Living with constant uncertainty is a skill honed by not having enough. Families with low income are forced to be resilient because the possibility of displacement is always looming. You can't get too connected to a place and sometimes to people because you might have to leave everything behind at any moment. Before we fully settled at St. James with our new baby, a letter was tacked on our door, telling us that the apartment couldn't accommodate three people, and we would have to leave. We had only weeks, but we found a two-bedroom apartment just outside of downtown on Jefferson Avenue. The rent was higher even though it was closer to some of the city's most dilapidated hotels, where drug dealers like my boyfriend set up to meet an endless stream of customers.

This was just another in a series of abrupt moves for us. A permanent address was a luxury. Decades later, in 2023, tenants of St. James Terrace received a similar letter on their doors. This time, it told them they had thirty days to pack their belongings and vacate the apartments. A new company had purchased the property and planned to do extensive renovations. They would not be renewing leases. One tenant, who had lived there for more than ten years, said it was like he "got hit by a truck."[8] In 2023, Newport News had the highest number of evictions in the state, and according to data from Princeton University's national Eviction Lab, it is among the nation's top evicting cities.[9]

It's challenging to give a full picture of how big of a problem housing insecurity in America actually is because we lack a standardized definition for it. So we measure it in different ways, like assessing the cost of housing, overcrowding in households, number of moves, and quality of housing. Homelessness—having no place to live—is considered the most severe form of housing insecurity. Even when we slice the crisis into these smaller parts, the picture is bleak. According to HUD, households are considered cost-burdened when they spend more than 30 percent of their income on their rent, mortgage, and other housing expenses. In 2023, nearly half of all renter households—more than twenty-one million—spent over 30 percent of their income on housing.[10] Renters with extremely low income pay even more. Forty-two percent of extremely low-income renters in DC spend 80 percent or more of their income on rent.[11]

There is no state or county in America in which a renter working full-time at minimum wage can afford a two-bedroom apartment.[12] None. California has the highest housing wage, meaning an individual would have to make $47.38 per hour or work 118 hours per week at the state's current minimum wage of $16 per hour in order to afford a two-bedroom rental home.[13] Working 118 hours would leave them with only 50 hours in the week, or 7.14 hours per day, to sleep, care for loved ones, commute, prepare and eat meals, and go to doctor's appointments, let alone read a book. In DC, an individual would have to make $39.33 per hour or work ninety hours per week at the District's current minimum wage of $17.50 to afford a two-bedroom rental home.

While housing unaffordability is a multifaceted problem, two of the most significant contributors are increased cost and lagging income. Housing costs have soared over the years, and income hasn't grown at the same rate. In 1960, renters spent less than a fifth of their income on rent. Even after adjusting for inflation, the median rent is up 75 percent from sixty years ago while the median renter income has increased by less than 15 percent.[14] Owning a home is also more difficult today than it was sixty years ago. When adjusted for inflation, a 1960 median house would cost just $104,619 in 2020 dollars compared to the actual cost of a median home for that year of $240,500. In other words, housing costs have increased by 129 percent. But during that same period, median household income increased by only 39 percent. After adjusting a median

1960 income for inflation, the earnings would be $49,232 in 2020 dollars compared to an actual median income for that year of $68,703.[15] Most Americans simply don't make enough money to keep up with rising housing costs. There *is* a share of the population that has seen significant increases in their income, though. Since 1980, the top 5 percent of the most affluent families in America have seen their income grow faster, further widening the gap of income and wealth inequality.[16]

Race and gender disparities in earnings exacerbate the housing affordability crisis. In 2023, white households had a median income of $89,050 compared to Hispanic households of $65,540 and Black households of $56,490—the lowest among all racial and ethnic groups.[17] When rent and home costs soar, and discrimination keeps earnings lower, people of color are less likely to afford housing. In forty-five states, Black renters have greater affordability challenges than their white counterparts. Discriminatory lending has resulted in Black and Latino borrowers frequently having higher mortgage rates.[18] In Colorado, which boasted the highest 2024 median housing sale price of $1,560,000 (in Edwards, Colorado),[19] 41 percent of Black homeowners spend more than 30 percent of their income on housing, compared to just 24 percent of white homeowners. A 2025 study *Displaced by Design* by the National Community Reinvestment Coalition found that gentrification—when urban development transforms a neighborhood from low to high value—has disproportionately displaced Black residents in major US cities because they can no longer afford the newly developed housing.[20]

Women, on average, earn 82 cents to every dollar made by men, and they also carry a heavier burden of housing costs, especially single mothers.[21] In 2021, nearly half of single women raising children who identified as Black, Native, Asian American and Native Hawaiian/Pacific Islander (AANHPI), or Latina were severely cost-burdened, meaning they spent more than 50 percent of their income on rent.[22] A Yale University study found that single women pay approximately 2 percent more than single men when buying a home, and they sell it for 2 percent less.[23] This crisis isn't new. In fact, it's been on presidential agendas for decades. In June 1946, while on his campaign trail, President John F. Kennedy gave a speech in Boston, Massachusetts, on the national housing crisis: "The right to a good home is one of the noblest motives in the American way of life—it is inherent in the heart and soul of every American and should be the cornerstone of all public policy."[24] Eighty years later, housing is even more out of reach for Americans, particularly for the most oppressed and marginalized.

The pandemic exposed challenges that millions of families had been navigating long before 2020—overcrowded homes being just one of them. During quarantine, I had a Zoom call with one of our Scholars in the DC-area program. I asked her how she was holding everything together for her son and managing remote learning. One of her biggest challenges was something many others wouldn't understand: finding a place to sit with her laptop for virtual classes. She shared a one-bedroom apartment in DC with eight people, including her parents, siblings, and three-year-old son. The kitchen table was already crowded with others using it for meals and online learning, while counters were lined with appliances. The chairs and beds were uncomfortable for extended use, and there was nowhere outside the apartment she could go, especially with a toddler.

Not having enough space was proving to be a significant barrier to her ability to stay in college.

Overcrowding, defined as housing with more than one occupant per room, results in more than just discomfort or inconvenience. It affects people's physical and mental health. Diseases like tuberculosis, other respiratory infections, and mold-related illnesses are more likely to spread in overcrowded rooms. Poorly ventilated, crowded spaces also attract mites and roaches, which can trigger breathing problems. Increased levels of stress come with overcrowding, making it hard for adults to focus on work or school and sometimes contribute to behavioral issues and poor academic performance in children. But much like those who were forced to live in cramped kitchenettes in Chicago's Black Belt, many families today have little choice. High housing costs often force people—grandparents, siblings, aunts, uncles, parents, sometimes friends—to crowd into a small apartment or house to have a roof over their heads. Without doubling up, they might be on the street.

During the Great Recession, which lasted from 2007 to 2009, the number of households living in crowded conditions surged. In 2010, those numbers began to decline, but by 2017, the number of overcrowded rental households increased from fewer than 37 million to an estimated

43.4 million.[25] More children are experiencing the stress and health risks associated with living in overcrowded homes. The number of children living with another family or sleeping in a hotel or motel with others increased by 3 percent, or nearly 1,071,000 children, between the 2014–15 and 2015–16 academic years.[26] A Voices of Youth Count report found that from 2016 to 2017, 1.81 million young people in the US, ages thirteen to twenty-five, were couch surfing, meaning they were staying with friends or family for short or extended periods of time.[27]

Children of young parents are even more likely to be couch surfing or living with multiple people; teen pregnancy and housing insecurity are intertwined, and most shelters and service providers don't serve minor parents. A 2018 study found that approximately 1.1 million children had a young parent who experienced homelessness in the past year.[28] That was our story. At twenty and nineteen years old, my boyfriend and I had been housing insecure for a year before we moved into our apartment at St. James Terrace right before having our daughter. If we hadn't found it when we did, we would have likely been couch surfing or back at the Motel 6 to keep a roof over our heads.

Just as food is more than sustenance, a home is more than shelter. When it is filled with love and warmth, it is a lighthouse, guiding us back to ourselves, no matter how dark it is. And while home is made special by the people we share it with, the consistency of a place matters too. A familiar front porch. A worn third stair. A perfect window to sit and watch the snow fall silently. It is the place where love and loss unfolds, the place where we take shape. But families with few resources often struggle to maintain stable housing, whether it's in an apartment, a house, or even a neighborhood.

Between 2005 and 2010, half of all households living below the poverty line moved a least once. Children in families with low income are twice as likely as those from affluent families to experience frequent moves.[29] Most of the time, these moves are forced, meaning the families have little choice but to relocate. Reasons include eviction notices, landlord challenges, and property-related issues. Moves can also be triggered by job changes, family needs, neighborhood safety, and a lack of essential services offered in their current area. Children who move frequently are more likely to perform poorly in school, have their education disrupted, and experience behavioral problems. Research shows the long-term impacts of this type of housing insecurity: the more times people moved as children, the more likely they are to report lower life satisfaction and psychological well-being and fewer quality social relationships as adults.[30]

It's easy to hear the story of Taylor Homes and assume that dilapidated housing is rare today. That's partly because most well-resourced people never venture into low-income neighborhoods or homes to see it for themselves and partly because it seems improvements in building codes and standards over the years should have prevented poor living conditions. But if you sit and listen to a family who is struggling to pay the bills each month, you will hear horror stories. Before we moved into St. James Terrace, we were renting a room in a condemned house in a predominantly Black neighborhood in Norfolk, Virginia. We left because we had been living with a cavernous, dripping hole in the ceiling right above our bed caused by heavy rain during a major summer storm. The landlord refused to fix it, and when we refused to pay rent, she locked us out of the room, forcing us to start sleeping on my boyfriend's stepsister's couch. I never saw our belongings that were locked inside the apartment again.

It's not enough to just have a roof over your head. The quality of your home profoundly affects your ability to pursue your education, create strong social networks, stay physically and mentally healthy, and grow up strong. An estimated 45 million homes in the US have one or more health or safety hazards, such as leaking roofs or ventilation or insulation issues,[31] and 6.7 million of them lack basic necessities, like electricity, plumbing, and adequate heating, and had structural problems, like holes in the floor or cracks in the wall.[32]

This isn't just a public housing problem. Homeowners and renters of private, unsubsidized housing also suffer from substandard conditions. Unable to afford or do the necessary repairs, they're at the mercy of negligent landlords, lacking support and oversight from local authorities to ensure improvements. The less income you have, the more likely you are to live in poor-quality housing, and after centuries of racial discrimination in housing, lending, and real estate practices, being Black, Indigenous, or Latino increases your likelihood of living in deficient housing. In 2021, 5.7 percent of Black homeowners lived in inadequate housing, compared to 2.9 percent of white homeowners.[33] In that same year, 10.2 percent of Black renter households lived in inadequate housing, compared to 7.0 percent of white renter households.[34]

Homelessness is the most significant form of housing insecurity for families. With nowhere to live, it's a daily struggle to stay employed, go to school, take care of yourself physically and mentally, and have healthy relationships. More people than ever are experiencing homelessness for the first time. In 2023, nearly one million people across the US experienced homelessness for the first time, the highest number ever recorded. On any given night in Tennessee, more than nine thousand people have nowhere to sleep. In New York, it's more than one hundred thousand people. In Texas, it's twenty-seven thousand. On a single night in January 2023, approximately 17,385 families in the US were living on the street, in a car, or in another place not meant for human habitation.[35]

Families experiencing homelessness are usually headed by young, single mothers, with limited education and young children, who are often fleeing violence, have lost work, or simply can't afford their rent. With these increases in the number of people experiencing homelessness, there aren't enough shelter beds. The nonprofit Streetlight analyzed a 2023 national data snapshot of homelessness, alongside available shelter capacity data, and found a significant shelter gap across the United States, with an estimated two hundred thousand fewer year-round shelter beds than the number of people who need them.[36]

These are the many facets of housing insecurity that families in poverty must traverse in order to change their circumstances. They are far-reaching, persistent, colossal, and far more deep-seated in America's ascent than we want to believe. Ensuring mothers and fathers have a chance at upward mobility will require a significant investment in their housing stability—one that addresses when and how the crisis began.

Displacement is a part of America's birth story. A Google search might tell you that homelessness became a national problem in the 1870s, when urbanization, industrialization, and railroads encouraged swarms of young, white men to travel in search of jobs. But widespread homelessness actually started in the early 1600s, when colonists began stealing ancestral land from thousands of Native Americans and either killing them or forcing them to relocate to unfamiliar territory. It continued over the next two hundred years as millions of enslaved people were kidnapped from their homes in Africa and brought to English settlements to live in poor, crowded conditions and barred from owning property. It extended to 1942 and the forced relocation of nearly 120,000 American citizens and residents of Japanese descent from their homes on the West Coast to live in prison-like camps, surrounded by barbed wire. We saw it in the devastating aftermath of Hurricane Maria in Puerto Rico in 2017, one of the deadliest US natural disasters in over one hundred years, when the federal government withheld approximately $20 billion in disaster relief from the US territory, leaving more than three hundred thousand homes damaged or destroyed and thousands of families displaced.[37]

Something doesn't just begin when it affects a certain group of people. It *begins* when it *begins*. The true inception of housing insecurity in America was when colonists first stepped on North American soil, and that's why it is tightly woven into the tapestry of our systems, practices, and policies. This economic violence isn't the whole of America, but it is a big part of us, in all our chaotic, beautiful glory.

Kristina's story is one of the most painful examples of how resilient millions of parents must be if they want to give their children a better life. A mother who became pregnant at fourteen, a first-generation college student, and someone who grew up in the foster care system, Kristina has had to overcome insurmountable odds to not just get into college but to *survive*. Housing insecurity has always been a part of her life. Before she enrolled at Trinity Washington University in DC and joined our program, she lost access to her transitional housing and became homeless due to an unstable foster care environment. Her daughter, Key'Monie, which means "unique and creative," was still an infant, and together, they slept in the Union Station Metro in DC while dodging police, fearing they'd be separated. Kristina recalls having to bathe Key'Monie in the Metro station's public restroom sink.

Kristina exemplifies how much is required of people who are experiencing housing insecurity to apply to and enroll in college, never mind to graduate. They must overcome disruptions in their K–12 schooling, increased stress; possible health, academic, and behavioral issues; scattered networks of support; low-wage full- or part-time jobs; and limited financial resources for their education. Still, like Kristina, some make it to college, likely recognizing that a credential is one of the best ways to secure stable, safe housing. But too many college students are housing insecure as they work toward that credential.

In 2020, the Hope Center found that 48 percent of the 195,000 students they surveyed reported some form of housing insecurity in the past twelve months; 14 percent reported being homeless.[38] About half of survey respondents at two-year colleges and two in five at four-year colleges experienced housing insecurity. The most common challenge for students at both types of institutions was housing affordability—not being able to pay the full amount of their rent, mortgage, or utility bills. The numbers for students of color are staggering. Across two- and four-year institutions, the report found that 75 percent of Indigenous students, 70 percent of Black students, and 70 percent of American Indian/Alaska Native students had experienced food insecurity, housing insecurity, and/or homelessness in the previous twelve months.

Most college campuses mirror the crises we see across the country. The same is true for housing insecurity. About half of parents with low income in the US report not having enough money for food or their rent or mortgage compared to 17 percent of middle-income parents.[39] Parents in college are struggling similarly. The Hope Center's 2020 report on student parents revealed that 68 percent of student parents had been housing insecure in the previous year and 17 percent had been homeless in the previous year.[40] At Generation Hope, 31.6 percent of our Scholars in the DC area and 37.5 percent of our Scholars in New Orleans have uncertain housing situations.

In order to help them stay in college, we provide emergency funding with very few barriers to access and maintain a robust network of organizations and agencies to help keep a roof over their heads. We've called shelters to inquire about openings. We've helped fill out paperwork. We've driven students to interviews for housing programs. Some colleges have established food pantries to combat food insecurity, but they have struggled to find or create housing solutions for students who are housing insecure. Plans that would accommodate students with children are even slower to materialize. Only 8 percent of institutions across the country offer family housing, which means the vast majority of parents who want to earn a postsecondary credential have to provide their own housing off campus, and it's often farther away from campus than other off-campus housing.[41]

Representative Ritchie Torres is one of those success stories that might tempt people to think that anyone can make it out of public housing and poverty if they just work hard enough. He was the youngest member of the New York City Council and the first openly gay, Afro-Latino elected to Congress in 2021. Torres represents the poorest congressional district in the United States by median income. His experience growing up in poor conditions, including "mold and mildew, leaks and lead, without reliable heat and hot water in the winter," made him run for office. The public housing he called home was, ironically, across the street from a Trump golf course. On a podcast during his campaign, Torres said, "I remember wondering to myself at the time, 'What does it say that our society is willing to invest more in a gated, gilded golf course for Donald Trump than in the homes of Black and Brown low-income Americans?'"[42]

There may be no clearer picture of how we got here than an Afro-Latino child looking out the window of his dilapidated public housing apartment at one of the many glittering golf courses of a millionaire. The housing affordability crisis—like food insecurity, transportation insecurity, childcare affordability, college costs, and more—is solvable, but we have to *want* to solve it. We have to want it more than we want more lush, fancy golf courses.

British mathematician and physicist William Thomson, also known as Lord Kelvin, once said, "If you cannot measure it, you cannot improve it."[43] Right now, we lack a good measure for how big the housing affordability crisis is. Reversing it requires both a shared definition and a standardized measure, which would allow us to establish clear, publicly available benchmarks that will track progress and ensure accountability from policymakers. In their 2023 *Politico* article, "The First Step to Solving the Housing Crisis Might Be Simpler Than You Think," Yuliya Panfil and Sabiha Zainulbhai make the case that America didn't effectively deal with its unemployment problem until it established an unemployment rate.[44] They suggest similarly calculating a national housing loss rate through a rigorous survey of the number of people who lost their homes the prior month coupled with a measure of supply, including the number of new housing units. While this wouldn't fully capture all forms of housing insecurity, it's a start that could prompt more attention to and investments in housing insecurity.

Next, we need more housing, in all forms. Established in 2008 by the Housing and Economic Recovery Act (HERA), the Housing Trust Fund (HTF) is a federal program that provides block grants to states to help build, rehabilitate, and preserve affordable housing for extremely low-income households. As of 2024, about $3 billion from HTF had been allocated to states, but to house families with extremely low income, 6.8 million more affordable housing units are needed.[45] To better meet this need, Congress should expand the HTF, which would not only benefit extremely low-income renters but also make more market-rate housing available to higher-income renters.[46]

Mills Place at 1736 Rhode Island Avenue, NE, is a sixty-one-unit affordable housing complex in the Brookland neighborhood of Ward 5 in DC, not far from Generation Hope's old office. It was built with HTF funding received by the District. In the 2019 press conference to announce the project, Mayor Muriel Bowser said: "While we continue to make historic affordable housing investments here in the District, we know we can't address the growing housing crisis alone—the federal government also must step up. We appreciate the National Housing Trust Fund and urge Congress to expand federal programs that help our most vulnerable residents."[47]

Much like WIC and SNAP, federal affordable housing programs at HUD and the USDA provide critical support to families, yet they are constantly under threat from lawmakers. The Housing Choice Voucher Program, also known as Section 8, is the largest federal rental assistance program, offering vouchers to help families with low income, the elderly, and people with disabilities rent privately owned housing. Public housing programs continue to provide affordable housing to extremely low-income families. The Low-Income Housing Tax Credits (LIHTC) program provides tax incentives to developers to encourage the construction and rehabilitation of affordable rental housing. The Community Development Block Grants (CDBG) program provides funding to local communities to benefit low- and moderate-income residents, including housing repairs and homelessness prevention. The Section 504 Home Repair Loans and Grants program provides loans and grants to very-low-income homeowners in rural areas to make essential home repairs. These are just some examples of the vital programs that must be protected if we want to ensure families can experience economic mobility.

If we look at how Taylor Homes failed its residents, we see heartbreaking experiences, but we also see opportunities to do things differently. Families need housing solutions that go further than providing four walls. They should also help to disrupt centuries of segregation and discrimination that have caused housing insecurity in the first place. Residents need wraparound services that address their many barriers to leaving poverty—nutritious food, childcare access, quality K–12 education, after-school programs and community centers, reliable public transportation, career training and employment opportunities, and support in pursuing a postsecondary credential.

Colleges can become partners in these efforts by advocating for affordable housing in the community and on their campuses. They can track both the parenting *and* housing status of their students, working closely with housing-related nonprofits to recruit and refer students, raising awareness of housing resources available on and off campus, prioritizing student parents, who are the most housing insecure, in their emergency aid application process, and offering classes in low-income communities. As with every effort, families can lead the way in designing impactful interventions.

When a building falls, there is sadness, but there's also something in the rubble, something stirring beneath. Soon the excavators will come to life again, and the mounds of debris will be shoveled away, pile by pile, laying bare what has always been beneath—an opportunity to build again. A chance to erect something more beautiful, more precise, something that should have been there all along, something that others closer to it could always envision but were kept from making a reality. And here it is now, finally able to see the radiant sunshine and feel the vast open air. What a marvelous thing it is, to begin again.

CHAPTER 9

THE SCARS AND THE DREAM

More than twenty years ago, I slowly pushed a clattering shopping cart out through the lazy automatic doors of a Williamsburg Food Lion, with no groceries, just my hungry toddler looking up at me while I tried to figure out how we were going to eat that night. The long walk to my white station wagon was measured and surreal. Seconds before, I had stood at the cash register while the cashier told me, after trying my debit card several times, that it had been declined for about twenty dollars' worth of groceries. The people in line behind me were annoyed, checking their watches and peering ahead trying to figure out what was taking so long. I quietly told the cashier, "Never mind," abandoned the food Nerissa and I had just judiciously picked off the shelves, and made my way out to my car while Nerissa inspected her baby doll, telling her she needed to brush her hair when we got home. This was one of the hardest and loneliest nights of my life.

Living in scarcity can be incredibly isolating. You don't share things because you're too embarrassed to admit they happened or because no one will fully understand or because, in not talking about them, you think you can protect yourself from their happening again or haunting you. But burying and stifling our experiences doesn't stop them from impacting us, shaping us, and coloring the lens through which we see the world. This was a lesson I had to learn over time. I was once too scared to tell the grocery store story—not just the slow walk back to our car with an empty cart but the next part, which was the hours that followed—because I thought telling it would disqualify me from something. Maybe I wouldn't meet the criteria for a scholarship or a promotion or just a *chance*. The most difficult part of the story to tell isn't what happened at the cash register. It's what happened when we were back in our campus apartment: I made Nerissa some scrambled eggs and found her a lonely stick of string cheese in the refrigerator for dinner. She went to bed happy, her doll's hair neatly brushed. I went to bed hungry and cried.

The fight for economic justice may feel complicated and full of jargon, conflicting theories, and complex equations, but at its core, it's quite simple. Tonight, a mother or a father will cry in the dark, feeling completely alone, and we must find a way to make things better in a tangible, game-changing way. Yes, they need canned goods to put in their cabinets and a backpack full of school supplies to strap to their little one's back, but more than those things, they need us to *care*—not in a superficial or pitying way, but in an urgent and connected way that translates into large-scale shifts. They need us to care more about them and their children than we do about stock prices, liquidity ratios, and the discomfort that comes with disrupting the status quo. They need us to care enough to do things differently because we see them not as a problem to be fixed, a project to be completed, or a number in a dataset, but as a person who deserves basic human rights—the right to prosper, the right to learn, the right to work, the right to care for their family, the right to eat well, the right to have choices, and the right to create a home. All of the basic building blocks for a life and a future and a legacy. They need the very *best* of us. The part that celebrates their humanity, their brilliance, and their potential—all bound up together in ours.

As I write this, some of the most severe wildfires in California's history are devouring more than thirty-seven thousand acres of land. At least twenty-nine people have died, and more than 10,600 structures have been destroyed, including homes, along with people's livelihoods. Firefighters are working around the clock to stop the blazes, some traveling from other states and even countries to help. The world is watching, hoping for an end to the destruction, and making donations to assist the many people who have been impacted. There is an understandable urgency in moments like this. People need help. It's not appropriate to ask if they *deserve* help or if they should have made better choices to keep themselves out of harm's way or if they will squander the support they receive, using it for drugs. Asking these questions would just be wrong and heartless.

Poverty is a global crisis felt acutely here on American soil. It impacts every facet of our lives from insufficient access to food, clean water, healthcare, education, and shelter to increased violence and crime to disproportionate impacts of climate change to our inability to compete as a global leader. It is the fourth-highest cause of death in the United States.[1] One in six children under the age of five in the US are poor, the highest rate of any age group.[2] We could liken it to a tsunami or a wildfire devastating the livelihoods of thirty-seven million people in the US each day. It is urgent. People need help. It's not appropriate to ask if they *deserve* help or if they should have made better choices to keep themselves out of harm's way or if they will squander the support they receive or use it for drugs. Asking these questions would just be wrong and heartless and would ignore the reality that America ignited this blaze. Except we *do* ask these questions, and we allow the endless and fruitless discourse to delay aid or interventions. So the fire rages on.

Despite the devastating impacts of poverty, there is no urgency to helping people out of it. We don't see poverty in the way that we see wildfires because poverty disproportionately impacts people of color. It's more tolerable than a raging wildfire because we have been conditioned to believe that the people who are consumed by poverty, including children, somehow *deserve* it. This is one of the most horrific designs of racism—its dehumanization of whole communities, making it more palatable to deny people of their basic rights and protections. Race isn't merely a factor; it is a deadly tool of economic violence. And it isn't being wielded just for cruelty's sake. Activist, author, and cocreator of #BlackLivesMatter Alicia Garza said: "I learned that racism, like most systems of oppression, isn't about bad people doing terrible things to people who are different from them but instead is a way of maintaining power for certain groups at the expense of others."[3] Racism and poverty are driven by a desperation to hold on to power, and the underbelly of needing to maintain power is the fear of losing it. That fear keeps the fire burning, stagnates progress, and holds millions of families in the constant paralysis of survival.

It will take a myriad of things to ensure all families have what they deserve to grow and thrive—some of which I've outlined in this book. We have to strengthen the safety net, with far-reaching and well-funded supplemental food programs, more affordable and quality housing, accessible healthcare, paid family leave, and expanded, high-quality childcare. We need to increase the minimum wage and create more better-paying jobs. We need comprehensive and affordable public transportation that connects low-income communities to employment and educational opportunities. We need better processes for ensuring funds are funneled to those who need it most, more realistic determinants of need that capture everyone who is truly struggling, and measures that prevent states from stockpiling or bottlenecking dollars. We need to acknowledge that poverty stems from deep-seated, long-standing racism and discrimination and do the hard, uncomfortable work of identifying it in our various systems and uprooting it. Otherwise we will continue to repeat our past mistakes.

And we must expand educational opportunities so people can grow their skills and enter family-sustaining careers that they're passionate about and that benefit all of us. It's the unseen piece of the puzzle. But legislation that ensures parents have access to a postsecondary credential is vital if we want families to climb the ladder, with lasting, generational impacts. The children of these parents will be more likely to go to college and succeed in a career themselves, halting generational cycles of poverty. This puzzle piece challenges our biases about who deserves to be in a classroom and confronts the notion that women should focus solely on child rearing not their education. It goes against the welfare queen trope so ingrained in our policies and public discourse—that mothers, particularly Black mothers, don't want to work hard and pursue their education. It opposes the negative stereotypes that fathers, particularly Black and Latino fathers, aren't engaged in their children's lives or committed to their own learning. It upends the belief that college should be a place for the privileged few and instead invites institutions to open their doors in ways they never have before.

To make college a viable option for more parents across the country, we'll need various federal- and state-level policy changes. We'll also need higher ed institutions to drive their own critical transformations. Nationwide, 40 percent of student parents don't feel welcome on their campuses,[4] which means many of these environments continue to perpetuate discriminatory and harmful practices, making parents feel out of place, especially Black, Latino, and Indigenous parents.

To start, colleges must know how many of their students are also parents. Just as understanding the magnitude of our country's housing crisis requires accurate data, each school needs a clear picture of how many of their students are raising children while pursuing their education. Without this data, they're missing vital information on a significant portion of their student body. Nationally, about 15 percent of students at four-year schools and 30 percent of students at community colleges are parenting.[5] For a community college with forty thousand students, that means twelve thousand of them might be balancing caregiving with their studies.

Next, colleges must examine their policies through a parenting lens. Schools have adopted policies from a higher education system never intended to educate women, students of color, students with low income, first-generation students, and certainly not students with children. Policies requiring freshmen to live in dorms or banning children from campus can make going to college as a parent incredibly difficult and, at times, impossible. Then, institutions of higher education must go beyond family-inclusive policies to examine their hiring and training practices, ensuring that all faculty and staff are sensitive to the needs of parenting students and understand how to support them. A college president championing student-parent inclusion is game-changing, but it doesn't prevent a professor from penalizing a father for turning in an assignment late because his toddler was sick for a week.

Finally, colleges and universities must ensure their culture communicates that parents aren't just tolerated but welcomed and celebrated. Simple things like providing high chairs in the dining halls or images of student parents with their children on the school website can send a powerful message to parents: "You *belong* here."

Colleges cannot be silent partners in opening doors to prosperity for families. Policymakers working to advance legislation at the state and local level will need allies. We see powerful things happen when key partners join forces. In 2022, a coalition helped California pass AB 2881, which granted student parents priority class registration to accommodate their demanding schedules. In 2024, a collective effort also helped to get the Greater Accessibility, Information, Notice, and Support (GAINS) for Student Parents Act passed. This act requires all public colleges and universities in California to improve financial aid accessibility for student parents and equips colleges to better identify and support them. In 2023, various groups in Texas came together to successfully advocate for several bills that enhance support for student parents by not only increasing assistance but also codifying their rights, ensuring that all colleges and universities are equipped to meet their unique needs. These legislative wins are possible only when we mobilize to rally support from lawmakers and create spaces where parents feel supported in sharing their powerful lived experiences to drive policy changes.

The pathway out of poverty can only be cleared—and forged—when we all are involved and recognize parents in poverty as capable and worthy. In this work, uniting across sectors and divides and amplifying stories of struggle that the world tells us to bury deep down inside are some of our most formidable superpowers.

That was the last time I pushed an empty grocery cart out to my car in a supermarket parking lot. It wasn't the last night I struggled, or the last night I cried, but that particular experience never happened to me—to us—again. Still, as fleeting as it was, it changed me. It took a chunk out of me. I saw the world differently, and I was reminded of how the world saw me. It is one of many scars that only I can see, and sometimes, like tracing a darkened scuff on a knee left from a fall years ago, my mind will find it, a whispered memory reminding me that perfection isn't as interesting as triumph, that love and joy in the face of adversity exhibit the greatest power of all. So I no longer see it as a flaw or something to be hidden. I'm not afraid to share it. It's one of my many war wounds, and I am a warrior. Anyone who has come through adversity is. Over the years, my battle scars have taught me that the dream was never to be perfect or to just survive. It was—and is—to understand our experiences as the things that reshape us and to revel in our ability to heal, to evolve, and to get up again.

During a panel discussion at the Connecticut Forum in 2001, author Toni Morrison was asked by an audience member how to survive whole in a world where we're all victims of something. She answered: "Sometimes you don't survive whole, you just survive in part. But the grandeur of life is that attempt. It's not about that solution. It is about being as fearless as one can, and behaving as beautifully as one can under completely impossible circumstances."[6] America has its scars and its parts. It is a tapestry of haunting imperfections and defiant joy, ever evolving, ever searching for itself. We trace the scars with our fingers to remember, and we find the courage to stretch new threads tightly on the loom, unsure of what the final arras will be. We won't live to see it whole, but we are committed to doing our part to get it there—for ourselves, for each other, for the little ones. And perhaps this is the true dream of America, the *attempt*, in all its beauty, complexity, and grandeur.

ACKNOWLEDGMENTS

I wrote this book in a time of upheaval for me, for all of us. Some days, I had so much to say that I wrote into the night, nearly falling asleep at the keyboard. Other days, a persistent heaviness made the words elusive. But sharing this project with the world has been a gift of expression and healing. Through every season of this journey, my community has been my anchor, encouraging me, pouring into me, motivating me, holding me, and reminding me that there is still so much boundless, radiant joy everywhere. That, too, has been an invaluable gift.

To my five beautiful children, Nerissa, Naya, Donte Jr., Drew, and Devin, you inspired me to write *and* made it hard to finish each chapter all at the same time, but I have fallen more in love with you every day. I cherish who you are now and who you are becoming, and I'm fighting to create a better world that deserves you. To my mom, Nancy, thank you for everything. So much of who I am as a mother comes from your gentle, unconditional love. I pray that your legacy of tenderness is imprinted on my little ones always.

To my literary agent, Joanne, thank you for showing up for me, believing in my ideas, and caring beyond the confines of this book. To the Beacon team, including my editor, Haley, I'm forever grateful for your help in bringing another one of my books to life. To everyone who tolerated my endless wordsmithing of this title (I do love where we landed), thank you for your patience with my middle-of-the-night texts. To Meron and Rebecca for always making me feel like I could write a hundred books . . . and run for president.

To my Generation Hope community, I am so thankful to be in the trenches with you. Thank you to our dedicated staff for doing the hard work every day, driving our mission forward, ensuring that families can realize their dreams. I hope you know I always see you. Thank you to our National Board and our Local Advisory Boards for dismantling the barriers that hinder those we serve and for standing with us as we dare to reshape the world. Thank you to our Scholars, Fellows, every student parent whose path has intertwined with ours, and those we have yet to meet. You inspire us. On the hardest days, it's the echoes of your triumphs and challenges that keep us going. To our partner institutions and organizations, from our FamilyU colleges to our coalition allies, thank you for locking arms with us and for being steadfast through all the storms we have faced and continue to face. Thank you to our volunteers, whether reading a book to a toddler or mentoring a Scholar, your time and talents will ripple through generations. To our funders and donors, this life-altering work, this tapestry of hope, would not exist without your investment, your unwavering belief in our vision, and your spirit of innovation.

And thank God for the strong sisterhood that carried me through this time just as sisterhood has carried the world through everything. You showed up for me, celebrated with me, laughed with me, checked on me, cried with me, and helped me carve out sacred rest. You sang my heart song back to me, and your love has been medicinal.

Lastly, thank you for taking the time to read this book. We are now companions, you and me. Now go and *do something* about what has stayed with you. And don't forget to *breathe*.

NOTES

CHAPTER 1: PROXIMITY AND THE CASSEROLE MINISTRY

1. L. B. Finer and J. M. Philbin, "Sexual Initiation, Contraceptive Use and Pregnancy Among Young Adolescents," *Pediatrics* (2013), doi:10.1542/peds.2012.3495, https://www.guttmacher.org/journals/psrh/2013/09/among-those-aged-12-and-younger-sexual-activity-uncommon.

2. Marleen van der Ree, Ingrid FitzGerald, and Jo Sauvarin, *Report on the Regional Forum on Adolescent Pregnancy, Child Marriage, and Early Union in South-East Asia and Mongolia*, UNFPA and UNICEF, 2018, https://www.unicef.org/eap/media/3696/file/Adolescent%20pregnancy.pdf.

3. Fact Forward, "The High Costs of Teen Pregnancy," press release, August 5, 2019, https://www.factforward.org/news/high-costs-teen-pregnancy.

4. Olivia Marshall, "The Drop Out Crisis and Teen Pregnancy," *Progressive Policy Institute* (blog), June 29, 2011, https://www.progressivepolicy.org/the-drop-out-crisis-and-teen-pregnancy/.

5. Health and Human Services, "Poverty Guidelines," https://aspe.hhs.gov/topics/poverty-economic-mobility/poverty-guidelines, accessed January 20, 2025

6. US Census Bureau, "National Poverty in America Awareness Month: January 2025," press release, January 2025, https://www.census.gov/newsroom/stories/poverty-awareness-month.html.

7. NFL, "Top 10 Largest-Capacity College Football Stadiums," https://www.nfl.com/photos/top-10-largest-capacity-college-football-stadiums-0ap1000000214278#16188a4d-ef72–4d6f-8e7f-ab0428b13246, accessed January 20, 2025.

8. Areeba Haider and Justin Schweitzer, "The Poverty Line Matters, but It Isn't Capturing Everyone It Should," Center for American Progress, March 5, 2020, https://www.americanprogress.org/article/poverty-line-matters-isnt-capturing-everyone/.

9. Celine-Marie Pascale, "Why the Federal Poverty Line Doesn't Begin to Tell the Story of Poverty in the U.S.," op-ed, *Los Angeles Times*, September 24, 2021, https://www.latimes.com/opinion/story/2021–09–24/federal-poverty-level-us-families.

10. World Bank Group, "GDP (US$)," https://data.worldbank.org/indicator/NY.GDP.MKTP.CD?most_recent_value_desc=true, accessed January 20, 2025.

11. OECD, "Poverty Rate," https://data.oecd.org/inequality/poverty-rate.htm, accessed January 20, 2025.

12. Jessica Semega, Melissa Kollar, Emily A. Shrider, and John F. Creamer, *Income and Poverty in the United States: 2019*, US Census Bureau, September 2020 (revised September 2021), https://www.census.gov/content/dam/census/library/publications/2020/demo/p60–270.pdf.

13. "Child Well-Being in Single-Parent Families," Annie E. Casey Foundation (blog), August 1, 2022 (updated April 6, 2024), https://www.aecf.org/blog/child-well-being-in-single-parent-families.

14. Annie E. Casey Foundation, Kids Count Data Center, https://datacenter.aecf.org/data/tables/55-families-with-related-children-that-are-below-poverty-by-family-type, accessed January 20, 2025.

15. Matthew Desmond, *Poverty, by America* (New York: Crown, 2024).

16. Oana Dumitru, "Half of Americans Say They Have Donated Money to Charity in the Past Year," YouGov-US, August 15, 2022, https://today.yougov.com/topics/society/articles-reports/2022/08/15/half-americans-donate-money-charity-past-year-poll.

17. Camilla A. Lehr, David R. Johnson, Christine Bremer, and Anna Cosio, "What Do We Know About Who Drops Out and Why?" *AdLit*, https://www.adlit.org/topics/dropout-prevention/what-do-we-know-about-who-drops-out-and-why, accessed May 7, 2025.

18. Drug Policy Alliance, *Rethinking the "Drug Dealer,"* December 17, 2019, https://drugpolicy.org/drugsellers.

19. Olga Khazan, "How Welfare Reform Left Single Moms Behind," *The Atlantic*, May 12, 2014, https://www.theatlantic.com/business/archive/2014/05/how-welfare-reform-left-single-moms-behind/361964/.

20. Katie Wright, "5 Things to Know About Single Mothers in Poverty: A Look at the Challenges Facing These Mothers and Their Families," Center for American Progress, May 11, 2012, https://www.americanprogress.org/article/5-things-to-know-about-single-mothers-in-poverty/.

21. Martin Luther King Jr., *Strength to Love* (Boston: Beacon Press, 2019), 25.

22. Martha Kempner, "Poverty Causes Teen Parenting, Not the Other Way Around," Rewire Newsgroup, April 29, 2013, https://rewirenewsgroup.com/2013/04/29/poverty-causes-teen-parenting-not-the-other-way-around/.

23. Tara O'Neill Hayes, "Incarceration and Poverty in the United States," American Action Forum, June 30, 2020, https://www.americanactionforum.org/research/incarceration-and-poverty-in-the-united-states/.

24. "Facing the School Dropout Dilemma," American Psychological Association, 2012, https://www.apa.org/pi/families/resources/school-dropout-prevention.

25. "Changing Illiteracy in the U.S. with Early Initiatives," Comic Relief, November 1, 2019, https://rednoseday.org/news/changing-illiteracy-and-poverty-in-america.

26. Martina Igini, "10 Powerful Nelson Mandela Quotes on Poverty, Inequality, and the Environment," Earth.org, July 18, 2022, https://earth.org/nelson-mandela-day-quotes/, accessed January 20, 2025.

27. Areeba Haider, "The Basic Facts About Children in Poverty," Center for American Progress, January 12, 2021, https://www.americanprogress.org/article/basic-facts-children-poverty/.

28. Loy Azalia and Emma Mehrabi, *The State of America's Children 2021*, Children's Defense Fund, https://www.childrensdefense.org/state-of-americas-children/soac-2021-child-poverty/.

29. "Social Determinants and Eliminating Disparities in Teen Pregnancy," Centers for Disease Control and Prevention, http://medbox.iiab.me/modules/en-cdc/www.cdc.gov/teenpregnancy/about/social-determinants-disparities-teen-pregnancy.htm, accessed January 20, 2025.

30. Health and Human Services, Office of Population Affairs, "Data and Statistics on Adolescent Sexual and Reproductive Health," https://opa.hhs.gov/adolescent-health/adolescent-sexual-and-reproductive-health/data-and-statistics-on-adolescent-sexual-and-reproductive-health, accessed January 20, 2025.

31. Katherine Schaeffer, "6 Facts About Economic Inequality in the U.S.," Pew Research Center, February 7, 2020, https://www.pewresearch.org/fact-tank/2020/02/07/6-facts-about-economic-inequality-in-the-u-s.

32. Sharice Davis, Cat Goughnour, and Lillian Singh, *Exploring Racial Economic Equity in Workforce Development*, Prosperity Now, July 2020, https://prosperitynow.org/sites/default/files/resources/Exploring-Racial-Economic-Equity-in-Workforce%20Development.pdf.

33. Harry J. Holzer, "The CEA Training Report: Very Wide of the Mark," *Skills Blog*, National Skills Coalition, August 13, 2019, https://nationalskillscoalition.org/blog/industry-engagement/the-cea-training-report-very-wide-of-the-mark/.

34. J. McFarland, B. Hussar, X. Wang, J. Zhang, K. Wang, A. Rathbun, A. Barmer, E. Forrest Cataldi, and F. Bullock Mann, *The Condition of Education 2018*, NCES, May 23, 2018, https://nces.ed.gov/programs/coe/pdf/Indicator_CPA/coe_cpa_2018_05.pdf.

35. Education Trust, *Access to Success in America: Critical Roles for Higher Education*, April 2015, https://edtrust.org/wp-content/uploads/2014/09/ca.oakland.WASC_.april_.pdf.

36. Haider, "The Basic Facts About Children in Poverty."

37. Kat Tretina, "Is College Worth the Cost? Pros vs. Cons," Nasdaq, December 29, 2020, https://www.nasdaq.com/articles/is-college-worth-the-cost-pros-vs.-cons-2020–12–29.

38. Caroline Griswold Short, Nicole Lynn Lewis, and Reginald Grant, *Higher Together: The Impact of a College Degree for Young Parents*, Generation Hope, May 2020, https://www.generationhope.org/alumni-report-2022.

39. Catherine Hensly, Chaunté White, and Lindsey Reichlin Cruse, *Re-Engaging Student Parents to Achieve Attainment and Equity Goals*, Institute for Women's Policy Research, July 2021, https://iwpr.org/iwpr-publications/re-engaging-student-parents-to-achieve-attainment-and-equity-goals/.

40. Monticello, "Jefferson Quotes & Family Letters," https://tjrs.monticello.org/letter/1283, accessed January 20, 2025.

41. University of Virginia, "Jefferson's Masterpiece," https://www.virginia.edu/visit/grounds, accessed January 20, 2025.

42. Frederick Rudolph, *The American College and University: A History*, 2nd ed. (Athens: University of Georgia Press, 1991).

43. Jaeah Lee, "Uncovering the Painful Truth About Racism on Campus," *Mother Jones*, November 20, 2015, https://www.motherjones.com/politics/2015/11/racism-campus-protests-mizzou-yale-craig-wilder/.

44. Antony P. Carnevale and Jeff Strohl, *Separate and Unequal: How Higher Education Reinforces the Intergenerational Reproduction of White Racial Privilege*, Georgetown University Center on Education and the Workforce, July 2013, http://cew.georgetown.edu/wp-content/uploads/SeparateUnequal.FR_.pdf.

45. William & Mary, "A Brief History," https://www.wm.edu/sites/100yearsofwomen/anniversary-story/brief-history/index.php, accessed January 20, 2025.

46. Lindsey Reichlin Cruse, Tessa Holtzman, Barbara Gault, David Croom, and Portia Polk, *Parents in College by the Numbers*, Institute for Women's Policy Research and Ascend, Aspen Institute, April 2019, https://ascend.aspeninstitute.org/resources/parents-in-college-by-the-numbers/.

47. Claire Wladis, "Opinion: Many Student-Parents Drop Out Because They Don't Have Enough Time for Their Schoolwork, Research Shows," *Hechinger Report*, July 24, 2018, https://hechingerreport.org/opinion-many-student-parents-drop-out-because-they-dont-have-enough-time-for-their-schoolwork-research-shows/.

48. GAO, "Higher Education: More Information Could Help Student Parents Access Additional Federal Student Aid," August 20, 2019, https://www.gao.gov/products/gao-19–522.

CHAPTER 2: RACE AND TINY SPARKS

1. Andre M. Perry, Anthony Barr, and Carl Romer, *The True Costs of the Tulsa Race Massacre: 100 Years Later*, Brookings Institution, May 28, 2021, https://www.brookings.edu/articles/the-true-costs-of-the-tulsa-race-massacre-100-years-later/.

2. "Klansville U.S.A.: The First Resurgence," *American Experience*, PBS, https://www.pbs.org/wgbh/americanexperience/features/klansville-resurgence/, accessed May 7, 2025.

3. Larry O'Dell, "Ku Klux Klan," *The Encyclopedia of Oklahoma History and Culture*, January 15, 2010, https://www.okhistory.org/publications/enc/entry?entry=KU001.

4. Thomas James Sharp to Joseph Anthony Sharp, June 28, 1921, Tulsa Historical Society & Museum, Tulsa, OK, https://www.tulsahistory.org/wp-content/uploads/2018/11/2021.170.001.pdf.

5. Nuria Martinez-Keel, "'A Conspiracy of Silence': Tulsa Race Massacre Was Absent from Schools for Generations," *EducationWeek* and *The Oklahoman*, May 26, 2021, https://www.edweek.org/teaching-learning/a-conspiracy-of-silence-tulsa-race-massacre-was-absent-from-schools-for-generations/2021/05.

6. Oklahoma Commission to Study the Tulsa Race Riot of 1921, *Tulsa Race Riot: A Report*, February 28, 2001, https://www.okhistory.org/research/forms/freport.pdf.

7. Dreisen Heath and Laura Pitter, *The Case for Reparations in Tulsa, Oklahoma: A Human Rights Argument*, Human Rights Watch, May 2020, https://www.hrw.org/news/2020/05/29/case-reparations-tulsa-oklahoma#_Toc41573968.

8. Vincent Schilling, "How Marriage and Murder Were Used to Steal Osage Oil Riches," History.com, October 23, 2023, https://www.history.com/news/osage-murders-reign-terror-husbands-guardians.

9. Rebecca Onion, "America's Lost History of Border Violence," *Slate*, May 5, 2016, https://slate.com/news-and-politics/2016/05/texas-finally-begins-to-grapple-with-its-ugly-history-of-border-violence-against-mexican-americans.html.

10. Brandon Zang, "What Happened at the Rock Springs Massacre?" *Encyclopedia Britannica*, October 2, 2020, https://www.britannica.com/story/what-happened-at-the-rock-springs-massacre.

11. Beau Driver, "1936 Border Closure," History of Colorado and Colorado Encyclopedia, https://coloradoencyclopedia.org/article/1936-border-closure, accessed January 20, 2025.

12. "Let's Not Repeat History: Lessons Learned from Federal Separation of Children and Families," op-ed, Partnership with Native Americans, July 12, 2018, https://nativepartnership.org/blog/history-culture-justice-category/op-ed-lets-not-repeat-history-lessons-learned-from-federal-separation-of-children-and-families/.

13. Ketanji Brown Jackson, "'A Tragedy for Us All': Ketanji Jackson's Impassioned Affirmative Action Dissent," *The Guardian*, June 29, 2023, https://www.theguardian.com/commentisfree/2023/jun/29/kentanji-brown-jackson-affirmative-action-dissent.

14. Doug Irving, "What Would It Take to Close America's Black-White Wealth Gap?" RAND, May 9, 2023, https://www.rand.org/pubs/articles/2023/what-would-it-take-to-close-americas-black-white-wealth-gap.html.

15. Urban Institute, "Survey of Financial Characteristics of Consumers 1962 (December 31)," "Survey of Changes in Family Finances 1963," and "Survey of Consumer Finances 1983–2016," https://apps.urban.org/features/wealth-inequality-charts/img/Nine%20Charts%20All%20Charts.pdf.

16. Kevin McElrath and Michael Martin, *Bachelor's Degree Attainment in the United States: 2005 to 2019*, American Community Survey Briefs, February 2021, https://www.census.gov/content/dam/Census/library/publications/2021/acs/acsbr-009.pdf.

17. Matthew Desmond and Mustafa Emirbayer, *Race in America*, 2nd ed. (New York: W. W. Norton, 2020).

18. Marwah Abdalla, "What Black Women Should Know About Heart Disease," Columbia University Irving Medical Center, February 11, 2022, https://www.cuimc.columbia.edu/news/what-black-women-should-know-about-heart-disease.

19. "Black Americans 1929–1941," Encyclopedia.com, https://www.encyclopedia.com/education/news-and-education-magazines/black-americans-1929-1941, accessed January 20, 2025.

20. Peter Irons, "Jim Crow's Schools," *American Educator* (Summer 2004), https://www.aft.org/ae/summer2004/irons.

21. Peter Irons, "Jim Crow's Schools."

22. *U.S. News & World Report*, "Bethune-Cookman University Student Life," https://www.usnews.com/best-colleges/bethunecookman-university-1467/student-life, accessed January 20, 2025.

23. Office of Accreditation, Quality Control, Compliance and Institutional Effectiveness, *FACT BOOK 2020–2021*, 40th ed., Bethune-Cookman University, https://www.cookman.edu/ie/_files/2020-2021-fact-book.pdf, accessed January 20, 2025.

24. *U.S. News & World Report*, "Bethune-Cookman University Student Life."

25. National Center for Education Statistics, IPEDS, "Financial Aid: What Is the Percent of Undergraduate Students Awarded Pell Grants?" https://nces.ed.gov/ipeds/trendgenerator/app/answer/8/35, accessed January 20, 2025.

26. National Center for Education Statistics, Fast Facts, "Historically Black Colleges and Universities," https://nces.ed.gov/fastfacts/display.asp?id=667, accessed January 20, 2025.

27. Joseph R. Biden Jr., "Proclamation 10451—National Historically Black Colleges and Universities Week, 2022," American Presidency Project, September 16, 2022, https://www.presidency.ucsb.edu/documents/proclamation-10451-national-historically-black-colleges-and-universities-week-2022.

28. Susan T. Hill, *The Traditionally Black Institutions of Higher Education 1860–1982*, National Center for Education Statistics, https://nces.ed.gov/pubs84/84308.pdf, accessed January 20, 2025.

29. Lindsey Reichlin Cruse, Tessa Holtzman, Barbara Gault, David Croom, and Portia Polk, *Parents in College by the Numbers*, Institute for Women's Policy Research and Ascend, Aspen Institute, April 2019, https://ascend.aspeninstitute.org/resources/parents-in-college-by-the-numbers/.

30. Venicia Gray, Stephanie Green, Ariel Adelman, and Blen Asres, *Black Women's Maternal Health: A Multifaceted Approach to Addressing Persistent and Dire Health Disparities*, National Partnership for Women & Families, November 2023, https://nationalpartnership.org/report/black-womens-maternal-health/.

31. Mayo Clinic, "Premature Birth," March 22, 2024, https://www.mayoclinic.org/diseases-conditions/premature-birth/symptoms-causes/syc-20376730.

32. "Racism and Homelessness Are Inextricably Linked. Here's What We're Doing About It," Community Solutions (blog), February 7, 2020, https://community.solutions/race-and-homelessness-are-inextricably-linked-heres-what-were-doing-about-it/?gad_source=1&gclid=CjoKCQiAsvWrBhCoARIsAO4E6f_Y-_dfA8tj44NH3uh41ZfBZ74YJf6OTw_sP_EE9jv7bsXLnRbGPH4aAm7jEALw_wcB.

33. Head Start, "Caring for the Health and Wellness of Children Experiencing Homelessness," last updated June 3, 2024, https://eclkc.ohs.acf.hhs.gov/publication/caring-health-wellness-children-experiencing-homelessness.

34. EdTrust, "Early Childhood Data Visualization," April 1, 2021, https://edtrust.org/early-childhood-tool/.

35. Linda Darling-Hammond, "Unequal Opportunity: Race and Education," Brookings Institution, March 1, 1998, https://www.brookings.edu/articles/unequal-opportunity-race-and-education/.

36. Richard O. Welsh, "Why, Really, Are So Many Black Kids Suspended?" *EducationWeek*, August 19, 2021, https://www.edweek.org/leadership/opinion-why-really-are-so-many-black-kids-suspended/2021/08.

37. Steven Reinberg, "Race, Income Keeps Many Families from Letting Kids Play Sports," *Medical Xpress*, August 11, 2022, https://medicalxpress.com/news/2022-08-income-families-kids-sports.html.

38. Jennifer Dineen and Andrea Malek Ash, "Student Data Lead Black, Hispanic Parents to Action," Gallup (blog), November 28, 2023, https://news.gallup.com/opinion/gallup/544730/student-data-lead-black-hispanic-parents-action.aspx.

39. CBS News, "Teen Pregnancy Linked to Good Grades," May 13, 2002, https://www.cbsnews.com/news/teen-pregnancy-linked-to-good-grades/.

40. Eduardo Cuevas, "Why Aren't Teens Having Sex? Report Gives Top Reasons Why Fewer Teens Are Sexually Active," *USA Today*, December 14, 2023, updated

December 15, 2023, https://www.usatoday.com/story/news/health/2023/12/14/cdc-teen-sex-contraception-sti-pregnancy/71920197007/.

41. Mohamad Moslimani, Christine Tamir, Abby Budiman, Luis Noe-Bustamante, and Lauren Mora, "Facts About the U.S. Black Population," Pew Research Center, January 18, 2024, https://www.pewresearch.org/social-trends/fact-sheet/facts-about-the-us-black-population/.

42. Latoya Hill, Samantha Artiga, Usha Ranji, Ivette Gomez, and Nambi Ndugga, "What Are the Implications of the Dobbs Ruling for Racial Disparities?" KFF, April 24, 2024, https://www.kff.org/racial-equity-and-health-policy/issue-brief/what-are-the-implications-of-the-overturning-of-roe-v-wade-for-racial-disparities/.

43. CDC, "About Teen Pregnancy," May 15, 2024, https://www.cdc.gov/reproductive-health/teen-pregnancy/?CDC_AAref_Val=https://www.cdc.gov/teenpregnancy/about/index.htm.

44. University of Cincinnati, https://cech.uc.edu/about/be-historic/native-american-heritage-month.html, accessed January 20, 2025.

45. National Center for Education Statistics, "Undergraduate Enrollment," May 2023, https://nces.ed.gov/programs/coe/indicator/cha/undergrad-enrollment.

46. Marián Vargas and Kim Dancy, "College Affordability Still Out of Reach for Students with Lowest Incomes, Students of Color," IHEP, August 16, 2023, https://www.ihep.org/college-affordability-still-out-of-reach-for-students-with-lowest-incomes-students-of-color/.

47. *Journal of Blacks in Higher Education*, "A Severe Lack of Teacher Diversity in the Nation's K–12 Schools," December 26, 2022, https://jbhe.com/2022/12/a-sever-lack-of-diversity-in-teacher-diversity-in-the-nations-schools/.

48. UNCF, "Education Inequality: K–12 Disparity Facts," https://uncf.org/pages/k-12-disparity-facts-and-stats, accessed January 20, 2025.

49. Grace Manthey, "Indigenous Students Can Face Large Education Gaps. Here's How One School Is Trying to Close Them," ABC7 Los Angeles, November 23, 2021, https://abc7.com/native-american-education-indigenous-students-achievement-gaps-school/11263264/.

50. Claire Cain Miller and Francesca Paris, "New SAT Data Highlights the Deep Inequality at the Heart of American Education," *New York Times*, October 23, 2023, https://www.nytimes.com/interactive/2023/10/23/upshot/sat-inequality.html.

51. Curtis Bunn, "Report: Black People Are Still Killed by Police at Higher Rate Than Other Groups," NBC News, March 3, 2022, https://www.nbcnews.com/news/nbcblk/report-black-people-are-still-killed-police-higher-rate-groups-rcna17169.

52. Eli Cahan, "'We're Losing Our People': COVID Ravaged Indigenous Tribes in New Mexico. Did Uranium Mining Set the Stage?" *USA Today*, August 26, 2022, https://www.usatoday.com/story/news/health/2022/08/26/uranium-mining-may-have-put-new-mexico-indigenous-tribes-covid-risk/7886296001/.

53. Jinann Bitar, Gabriel Montague, and Lauren Ilano, "Faculty Diversity and Student Success Go Hand in Hand, So Why Are University Faculties So White?" Education Trust, December 1, 2022, https://edtrust.org/resource/faculty-diversity-and-student-success-go-hand-in-hand-so-why-are-university-faculties-so-white/.

54. Laura Spitalniak, "1 in 5 Black Students Face Discrimination in College, Survey Finds," Higher Ed Dive, February 9, 2023, https://www.highereddive.com/news/black-students-discrimination-in-college/642313/.

55. Cristobal de Brey et al., *Status and Trends in the Education of Racial and Ethnic Groups 2018* (Washington, DC: National Center for Education Statistics, 2019), https://nces.ed.gov/pubs2019/2019038.pdf.

56. Spitalniak, "1 in 5 Black Students Face Discrimination in College."

57. Megan Leonhardt, "Black Parents Without Child Care Are Twice as Likely to Suffer at Work," CNBC, July 7, 2020, https://www.cnbc.com/2020/07/07/black-parents-without-child-care-twice-as-likely-to-suffer-at-work.html.

58. Generation Hope, *National Student Parent Survey Results & Recommendations: Uncovering the Student Parent Experience and Its Impact on College Success* (Washington, DC: Generation Hope, 2020), https://www.generationhope.org/student-parents-report-2020.

59. Chimamanda Ngozi Adichie, *Americanah*, reprint ed. (New York: Vintage, 2014).

60. Nina Banks, "Black Women's Labor Market History Reveals Deep-Seated Race and Gender Discrimination," Economic Policy Institute, February 19, 2019, https://www.epi.org/blog/black-womens-labor-market-history-reveals-deep-seated-race-and-gender-discrimination/.

CHAPTER 3: GENDER AND OUR COMPANIONS

1. Brené Brown, "Shame v. Guilt," January 15, 2013, https://brenebrown.com/articles/2013/01/15/shame-v-guilt/, accessed April 6, 2025.

2. Judith Stadtman Tucker, "Motherhood, Shame and Society," Mothers Movement Online, http://www.mothersmovement.org/features/bbrown_int/bbrown_int_1.htm, accessed April 6, 2025.

3. Legal Momentum, "Women and Poverty in America," https://www.legalmomentum.org/women-and-poverty-america, accessed April 6, 2025.

4. Robin Bleiweis, Diana Boesch, and Alexandra Cawthorne Gaines, "Basic Facts About Women and Poverty," Center for American Progress, August 3, 2020, https://www.americanprogress.org/article/basic-facts-women-poverty/.

5. National Women's Law Center, *When Hard Work Is Not Enough: Women in Low-Paid Jobs*, April 2020, https://nwlc.org/wp-content/uploads/2020/04/Women-in-Low-Paid-Jobs-report_ES_pp01.pdf.

6. National Women's Law Center, *When Hard Work Is Not Enough*.

7. Bleiweis, Boesch, and Gaines, "Basic Facts About Women and Poverty."

8. US Government Accountability Office, *Women in the Workforce: The Gender Pay Gap Is Greater for Certain Racial and Ethnic Groups and Varies by Education Level*, December 15, 2022, https://www.gao.gov/products/gao-23–106041.

9. Bleiweis, Boesch, and Gaines, "Basic Facts About Women and Poverty."

10. National Women's Law Center, *When Hard Work Is Not Enough*.

11. Elise Gould, "Over 60% of Low-Wage Workers Still Don't Have Access to Paid Sick Days on the Job," Economic Policy Institute (blog), September 23, 2022, https://www.epi.org/blog/over-60-of-low-wage-workers-still-dont-have-access-to-paid-sick-days-on-the-job/.

12. Oxfam America, *The Low-Wage Worker Report: Inequality and the Failure of Corporate Influence on Our Workforce*, 2013, https://s3.amazonaws.com/oxfam-us/www/static/media/files/low-wage-worker-report-oxfam-america.pdf.

13. Oxfam America, *The Low-Wage Worker Report*.

14. Madeleine Kunin, "Family and Medical Leave Act Needs One More Word—Paid," *VTDigger*, February 5, 2013, https://vtdigger.org/2013/02/05/kunin-family-and-medical-leave-act-needs-one-more-word-paid/.

15. Najah Mills, "How Public Benefit Programs Are Blocking the Path to Economic Mobility for Student Parents," *The Grio*, April 28, 2023, https://thegrio.com/2023/04/28/how-public-benefit-programs-are-blocking-the-path-to-economic-mobility-for-student-parents/.

16. Bleiweis, Boesch, and Gaines, "Basic Facts About Women and Poverty."

17. Gene Falk and Patrick A. Landers, "The Temporary Assistance for Needy Families (TANF) Block Grant: Responses to Frequently Asked Questions," Congressional Research Service, April 1, 2024, https://sgp.fas.org/crs/misc/RL32760.pdf.

18. Robert A. Moffitt and Stephanie Garlow, "Did Welfare Reform Increase Employment and Reduce Poverty?" *Pathways: A Magazine on Poverty, Inequality, and Social Policy* (Winter 2018), https://inequality.stanford.edu/sites/default/files/Pathways_Winter2018_Employment-Poverty.pdf.

19. Ife Floyd et al., "TANF Policies Reflect Racist Legacy of Cash Assistance: Reimagined Program Should Center Black Mothers," Center on Budget and Policy Priorities, August 4, 2021, https://www.cbpp.org/research/income-security/tanf-policies-reflect-racist-legacy-of-cash-assistance.

20. Tim Naftali, "Ronald Reagan's Long-Hidden Racist Conversation with Richard Nixon," *The Atlantic*, July 30, 2019, https://www.theatlantic.com/ideas/archive/2019/07/ronald-reagans-racist-conversation-richard-nixon/595102/.

21. Gene Demby, "The Mothers Who Fought to Radically Reimagine Welfare," NPR, June 9, 2019, https://www.npr.org/sections/codeswitch/2019/06/09/730684320/the-mothers-who-fought-to-radically-reimagine-welfare.

22. Teresa Amott and Julie Matthaei, *Race, Gender, and Work: A Multicultural Economic History of Women in the U.S.* (Boston: South End Press, 1996).

23. Judith B. Bremner, "Black Pink Collar Workers: Arduous Journey from Field and Kitchen to Office," *Journal of Sociology & Social Welfare* 19, no. 3, art. 2 (1992), https://scholarworks.wmich.edu/jssw/vol19/iss3/2?utm_source=scholarworks.wmich.edu%2Fjssw%2Fvol19%2Fiss3%2F2&utm_medium=PDF&utm_campaign=PDFCoverPages.

24. Jacqueline Jones, *Labor of Love, Labor of Sorrow: Black Women, Work, and the Family from Slavery to the Present* (New York: Basic Books, 1985).

25. Nina Banks, "Black Women's Labor Market History Reveals Deep-Seated Race and Gender Discrimination," Economic Policy Institute, February 19, 2019, https://www.epi.org/blog/black-womens-labor-market-history-reveals-deep-seated-race-and-gender-discrimination/.

26. Kaitlyn Henderson, "How Do Employers Get Away with Paying Lower Wages?" Politics of Poverty, Oxfam America, March 22, 2022, https://politicsofpoverty.oxfamamerica.org/how-do-employers-get-away-with-paying-lower-wages/.

27. Bernie Sanders, "Sanders, Scott, 29 Democratic Senators, Introduce Legislation to Raise the Minimum Wage to $17 by 2028, Benefitting Nearly 28 Million Workers Across America," press release, July 25, 2023, https://www.sanders.senate.gov/press-releases/news-sanders-scott-29-democratic-senators-introduce-legislation-to-raise-the-minimum-wage-to-17-by-2028-benefitting-nearly-28-million-workers-across-america/.

28. Emily Ekins, "What Americans Think About Poverty, Wealth, and Work," Cato Institute, September 24, 2019, https://www.cato.org/publications/survey-reports/what-americans-think-about-poverty-wealth-work.

29. Marcella Bombardieri, "The Imperative to Support Single Mothers in College," Center for American Progress, July 19, 2018, https://www.americanprogress.org/article/imperative-support-single-mothers-college/.

30. Niall McCarthy, "Women Are Still Earning More Doctoral Degrees Than Men in the U.S.," *Forbes*, October 5, 2018, https://www.forbes.com/sites/niallmccarthy/2018/10/05/women-are-still-earning-more-doctoral-degrees-than-men-in-the-u-s-infographic/?sh=49dcfb3345b6.

31. Generation Hope, *National Student Parent Survey Results & Recommendations: Uncovering the Student Parent Experience and Its Impact on College Success* (Washington, DC: Generation Hope, 2020), https://www.generationhope.org/student-parents-report-2020.

32. Library of Congress, "Title IX of the Education Amendments of 1972: Resources from the Law Library," https://guides.loc.gov/title-IX-law-library-resources/legislative-path, accessed April 6, 2025.

33. George A. Akerlof and Janet L. Yellen, "An Analysis of Out-of-Wedlock Births in the United States," Brookings Institution, August 1, 1996, https://www.brookings.edu/articles/an-analysis-of-out-of-wedlock-births-in-the-united-states/.

34. Jo Jones and William D. Mosher, *Fathers' Involvement with Their Children: United States, 2006–2010*, National Health Statistics Reports, No. 71 (Hyattsville, MD: National Center for Health Statistics, 2013), https://www.cdc.gov/nchs/data/nhsr/nhsr071.pdf.

35. National Student Clearinghouse Research Center, "Current Term Enrollment Estimates," January 23, 2025, https://nscresearchcenter.org/current-term-enrollment-estimates/.

36. Richard V. Reeves, Eliana Buckner, and Ember Smith, "The Unreported Gender Gap in High School Graduation Rates," Brookings Institution, January 12, 2021, https://www.brookings.edu/articles/the-unreported-gender-gap-in-high-school-graduation-rates/.

37. National Center for Education Statistics, US Department of Education, "Table 322.20. Percentage of Persons 25 to 29 Years Old with Selected Levels of Educational Attainment, by Race/Ethnicity and Sex: Selected Years, 1940 Through 2021," Digest of Education Statistics, https://nces.ed.gov/programs/digest/d21/tables/dt21_322.20.asp?current=yes.

38. PNPI, "Men of Color Fact Sheet," January 2023, https://pnpi.org/wp-content/uploads/2023/01/MenOfColorFactSheet_Jan2023.pdf.

39. Susana Contreras-Mendez and Lindsey Reichlin Cruse, *Busy with Purpose: The Impact of COVID-19 on Essential Workers by Race, Gender, and Pay* (Washington, DC: Institute for Women's Policy Research, 2021), https://iwpr.org/wp-content/uploads/2021/03/Busy-With-Purpose-v2b.pdf.

40. Anne Hathaway, "Speech at the UN Official Commemoration of International Women's Day," UN Women, March 8, 2017, https://www.unwomen.org/en/news/stories/2017/3/speech-anne-hathaway-iwd-2017.

CHAPTER 4: MONEY AND BLOOD

1. "Violence," Merriam-Webster.com, https://www.merriam-webster.com/dictionary/violence, accessed April 6, 2025.

2. National Archives, "Findings on MLK Assassination," https://www.archives.gov/research/jfk/select-committee-report/part-2a.html, accessed April 6, 2025.

3. Ayanna Pressley, "2019 Boston Women's March, Jan. 21, 2019," Carrie Chapman Catt Center for Women and Politics, Archives of Women's Political Communication, March 4, 2022, https://awpc.cattcenter.iastate.edu/2022/03/04/2019-boston-womens-march-jan-21-2019/.

4. NAACP, "History of Lynching in America," NAACP, https://naacp.org/find-resources/history-explained/history-lynching-america, accessed September 2, 2025; Adam McCann, "Most & Least Educated States," WalletHub, February 10, 2025, https://wallethub.com/edu/e/most-educated-states/31075.

5. TalkPoverty, *Mississippi 2020 Report*, https://talkpoverty.org/state-year-report/mississippi-2020-report/index.html, accessed April 6, 2025.

6. Anne Price and Jhumpa Bhattacharya, *Mississippi Is America: How Racism and Sexism Sustain a Two-Tiered Labor Market in the US and Constrict the Economic Power of Workers in Mississippi and Beyond* (Oakland, CA: INSIGHT Center for Community Economic Development, 2020), https://insightcced.org/wp-content/uploads/2020/10/INSIGHT_Mississippi-Is-America-brief_3.pdf.

7. David Danelski, "Poverty Is 4th Greatest Cause of U.S. Deaths," UC Riverside News, April 17, 2023, https://news.ucr.edu/articles/2023/04/17/poverty-4th-greatest-cause-us-deaths.

8. David Brady, Ulrich Kohler, and Hui Zheng, "Novel Estimates of Mortality Associated with Poverty in the US," *JAMA Internal Medicine* 183, no. 7 (April 17, 2023): 718–19, https://jamanetwork.com/journals/jamainternalmedicine/fullarticle/2804032.

9. Matthew P. Rabbitt, Laura J. Hales, and Madeline Reed-Jones, "Food Security in the U.S.," USDA ERS, January 8, 2025, https://www.ers.usda.gov/topics/food-nutrition-assistance/food-security-in-the-u-s/.

10. Feeding America, "Child Hunger Facts," https://www.feedingamerica.org/hunger-in-america/child-hunger-facts, accessed April 6, 2025.

11. Century Foundation, "TCF Study Finds U.S. Schools Underfunded Nearly $150 Billion Annually," July 22, 2020, https://tcf.org/content/about-tcf/tcf-study-finds-u-s-schools-underfunded-nearly-150-billion-annually/.

12. Ariane Hegewisch, Cristy Mendoza, Miranda Peterson, and Martha Susana Jaimes, "State by State, Mothers Are Paid Much Less Than Fathers," IWPR, August 15, 2023, https://iwpr.org/state-by-state-mothers-are-paid-much-less-than-fathers/.

13. Leah Wang and Wanda Bertram, "New Data on Formerly Incarcerated People's Employment Reveal Labor Market Injustices," Prison Policy Initiative, February 8, 2022, https://www.prisonpolicy.org/blog/2022/02/08/employment/.

14. Claudia J. Coulton, Francisca Richter, Seok-Joo Kim, Robert Fischer, and Youngman Cho, "Poor Kindergarten Readiness Scores Are Linked to Substandard Housing and Neighborhood Conditions," Housing Matters, Urban Institute, August 16, 2016, https://housingmatters.urban.org/research-summary/poor-kindergarten-readiness-scores-are-linked-substandard-housing-and-neighborhood.

15. Dhruv Khullar and Dave A. Chokshi, "Health, Income, & Poverty: Where We Are & What Could Help," Health Affairs Forefront, Health Affairs, October 4, 2018, https://www.healthaffairs.org/content/briefs/health-income-poverty-we-could-help.

16. Kelly M. Hoffman, Sophie Trawalter, Jordan R. Axt, and M. Norman Oliver, "Racial Bias in Pain Assessment and Treatment Recommendations, and False Beliefs About Biological Differences Between Blacks and Whites," *Personality and Individual Differences* 98 (April 2016): 85–91, https://www.ncbi.nlm.nih.gov/pmc/articles/PMC4843483/.

17. Brad N. Greenwood, Rachel R. Hardeman, Laura Huang, and Aaron Sojourner, "Physician–Patient Racial Concordance and Disparities in Birthing Mortality for Newborns," *Proceedings of the National Academy of Sciences* 117, no. 35 (August 17, 2020), https://www.pnas.org/doi/10.1073/pnas.1913405117.

18. Office of the High Commissioner for Human Rights, United Nations, "Contempt for the Poor in US Drives Cruel Policies, Says UN Expert," June 4, 2018, https://www.ohchr.org/en/press-releases/2018/06/contempt-poor-us-drives-cruel-policies-says-un-expert?LangID=E&NewsID=23172.

19. Association of Public and Land-Grant Universities, "How Does a College Degree Improve Graduates' Employment and Earnings Potential?" https://www.aplu.org/our-work/4-policy-and-advocacy/publicuvalues/employment-earnings/, accessed April 6, 2025.

20. Association of Public and Land-Grant Universities, "How Do College Graduates Benefit Society at Large?" https://www.aplu.org/our-work/4-policy-and-advocacy/publicuvalues/societal-benefits/, accessed April 6, 2025.

21. Point2Homes, "Homeownership by Education in the US," https://www.point2homes.com/news/us-real-estate-news/homeownership-by-education-us.html, accessed April 6, 2025.

22. Michael T. Nietzel, "New Evidence Documents That a College Degree Pays Off—By a Lot," *Forbes*, January 15, 2020, https://www.forbes.com/sites/michaeltnietzel/2020/01/15/new-evidence-documents-that-a-college-degree-pays-off-by-a-lot/?sh=5ad7a4cf3a98.

23. Johanna Alonso, "Measuring Higher Ed's Benefits Beyond Earnings," *Inside Higher Ed*, August 30, 2023, https://www.insidehighered.com/news/students/careers/2023/08/30/study-shows-higher-ed-linked-kinder-healthier-citizens.

24. Sara Weissman, "New Analysis Finds Most Families Can't Cover College Costs," *Inside Higher Ed*, August 18, 2023, https://www.insidehighered.com/news/quick-takes/2023/08/18/new-analysis-finds-most-families-cant-cover-college-costs.

25. National Center for Education Statistics, US Department of Education, "Table 320. Educational Attainment of the Population 25 Years and Over, by Race/Ethnicity, Age, and Sex: Selected Years, 1940 Through 2007," Digest of Education Statistics, https://nces.ed.gov/programs/digest/d07/tables/dt07_320.asp.

26. Jennifer Ma, Sandy Baum, Matea Pender, and C. J. Libassi, *Trends in College Pricing 2017* (New York: College Board, 2017), https://research.collegeboard.org/media/pdf/trends-college-pricing-2017-full-report.pdf.

27. Annie Nova, "Pulitzer Prize-Winning Journalist Explains How College Became So Expensive," CNBC, October 27, 2022, https://www.cnbc.com/2022/10/27/pulitzer-prize-winning-journalist-explains-how-college-became-so-expensive.html.

28. Mark J. Perry, "Chart of the Day . . . or Century?" American Enterprise Institute, January 14, 2020, https://www.aei.org/carpe-diem/chart-of-the-day-or-century-3/.

29. Devin Fergus, "My Students Pay Too Much for College. Blame Reagan," *Washington Post*, September 2, 2014, https://www.washingtonpost.com/posteverything/wp/2014/09/02/my-students-pay-too-much-for-college-blame-reagan/.

30. Kamaron McNair, "How Much Student Loan Borrowers Owe in Every U.S. State—in One Map," CNBC, March 17, 2025, https://www.cnbc.com/2025/03/17/average-student-debt-balance-in-every-state.html.

31. Brittani Williams, Jinann Bitar, Portia Polk, and Andre Nguyen, *For Student Parents, the Biggest Hurdles to a Higher Education Are Cost and Finding Child Care* (Washington, DC: Education Trust, 2022), https://edtrust.org/wp-content/uploads/2014/09/For-Student-Parents-The-Biggest-Hurdles-to-a-Higher-Education-Are-Cost-and-Finding-Child-Care-August-2022.pdf.

32. National College Attainment Network (NCAN), "College Affordability," https://www.ncan.org/page/Affordability, accessed April 6, 2025.

33. Oxfam America, *The Low-Wage Worker Report: Inequality and the Failure of Corporate Influence on Our Workforce* (Boston: Oxfam America, 2013), https://s3.amazonaws.com/oxfam-us/www/static/media/files/low-wage-worker-report-oxfam-america.pdf.

34. Elizabeth Hyde, Margaret E. Greene, and Gary L. Darmstadt, "Time Poverty: Obstacle to Women's Human Rights, Health and Sustainable Development," *Journal of Global Health* (December 2020), https://www.ncbi.nlm.nih.gov/pmc/articles/PMC7688061/.

35. Claire Wladis, "College Students with Young Kids," *ASBMB Today*, January 29, 2022, https://www.asbmb.org/asbmb-today/careers/012922/college-students-with-young-kids.

36. Melanie Hanson, "Scholarship Statistics," EducationData.org, November 3, 2024, https://educationdata.org/scholarship-statistics.

37. Annie Nova, "$6 Billion in College Scholarships Are Awarded Each Year. Here's What You Need to Know About Applying," CNBC, April 4, 2023, https://www.cnbc.com/2023/04/04/everything-students-need-to-know-about-college-scholarships.html.

38. Raj Chetty, David J. Deming, and John N. Friedman, "Diversifying Society's Leaders? The Determinants and Causal Effects of Admission to Highly Selective Private Colleges," Opportunity Insights, October 2023, https://opportunityinsights.org/wp-content/uploads/2023/07/CollegeAdmissions_Paper.pdf.

39. Wesley Whistle, "Millennials and Student Loans: Rising Debts and Disparities," New America, https://www.newamerica.org/millennials/reports/emerging-millennial-wealth-gap/millennials-and-student-loans-rising-debts-and-disparities/, accessed April 6, 2025.

40. Ben Miller, "New Federal Data Show Student Loan Crisis for African American Borrowers," Center for American Progress, October 16, 2019, https://www.americanprogress.org/article/new-federal-data-show-student-loan-crisis-african-american-borrowers/.

41. Wesley Whistle, "Wealth Inequality and Higher Education: How Billionaires Could Make a Difference," *Forbes*, December 31, 2019, https://www.forbes.com/sites/wesleywhistle/2020/12/31/wealth-inequality-and-higher-education-how-billionaires-could-make-a-difference/?sh=541928b139db.

42. Whistle, "Wealth Inequality and Higher Education."

43. Chuck Collins, "Updates on Billionaire Pandemic Profiteering," Inequality.org, March 18, 2024, https://inequality.org/great-divide/updates-billionaire-pandemic/.

44. National Center for Education Statistics, US Department of Education, "Fast Facts: Educational Attainment of the U.S. Population," https://nces.ed.gov/fastfacts/display.asp?id=84, accessed April 6, 2025.

CHAPTER 5: CHILDCARE AND BREATHING

1. Sidney Madden, Sam Leeds, and Rodney Carmichael, "'I Want Us to Dream a Little Bigger': Noname and Mariame Kaba on Art and Abolition," SDPB, December 19, 2020, https://www.sdpb.org/2020–12–19/i-want-us-to-dream-a-little-bigger-noname-and-mariame-kaba-on-art-and-abolition.

2. Care.com, "How Much Does Child Care Cost?" January 29, 2025, https://www.care.com/c/how-much-does-child-care-cost/.

3. Donald L. Fixico, "When Native Americans Were Slaughtered in the Name of 'Civilization,'" History.com, A&E Television Networks, last updated February 18, 2025, https://www.history.com/articles/native-americans-genocide-united-states.

4. Ta-Nehisi Coates, "Slavery Made America," *The Atlantic*, June 24, 2014, https://www.theatlantic.com/business/archive/2014/06/slavery-made-america/373288/.

5. "'We Are Literally Slaves': An Early Twentieth-Century Black Nanny Sets the Record Straight," History Matters, https://historymatters.gmu.edu/d/80/, accessed April 6, 2025.

6. Carrie Gillispie, Caitlin Codella, Aaron Merchen, and Joseph Davis, *Equity in Child Care Is Everyone's Business* (Washington, DC: US Chamber of Commerce Foundation, 2021), https://chamber-foundation.files.svdcdn.com/production/documents/Equity_ChildCare_Final_web.pdf?dm=1694110498.

7. Claire Ewing-Nelson, *One in Five Child Care Jobs Have Been Lost Since February, and Women Are Paying the Price* (Washington, DC: National Women's Law Center, 2020), https://nwlc.org/wp-content/uploads/2020/08/ChildCareWorkersFS.pdf.

8. Gillispie, Codella, Merchen, and Davis, *Equity in Child Care Is Everyone's Business*.

9. Child Care Aware of America, "16,000 Child Care Providers Shut Down in the Pandemic. It's a Really Big Deal," February 9, 2022, https://info.childcareaware.org/media/16000-childcare-providers-shut-down-in-the-pandemic.-its-a-really-big-deal.

10. Gillispie, Codella, Merchen, and Davis, *Equity in Child Care Is Everyone's Business*.

11. Ewing-Nelson, *One in Five Child Care Jobs Have Been Lost Since February, and Women Are Paying the Price*.

12. Elise Gould, "Child Care Workers Aren't Paid Enough to Make Ends Meet," Economic Policy Institute, November 15, 2015, https://www.epi.org/publication/child-care-workers-arent-paid-enough-to-make-ends-meet/.

13. Care.com, "How Much Does Child Care Cost?"

14. Sarah Nzau and Tia Caldwell, "Access to Child Care for Student Parents," New America, September 28, 2023, https://www.newamerica.org/education-policy/edcentral/access-child-care-student-parents/.

15. Casey Eggleston, Yeris H. Mayol Garcia, Mikelyn Meyers, and Yazmin Garcia Trejo, "Child Care in the U.S.: Who Uses It and How Much Does It Cost?" US Census Bureau, November 29, 2023, https://www.census.gov/library/stories/2023/11/child-care.html.

16. Occupational Employment and Wage Statistics (OEWS) Tables, US Bureau of Labor Statistics, last modified April 2, 2025, https://www.bls.gov/oes/tables.htm.

17. OEWS Tables, US Bureau of Labor Statistics.

18. Lindsey Reichlin Cruse, Lashawn Richburg-Hayes, Amanda Hare, and Susana Contreras-Mendez, *Evaluating the Role of Campus Child Care in Student Parent Success* (Washington, DC: IWPR, 2021), https://iwpr.org/wp-content/uploads/2021/10/Evaluating-the-Role-of-Campus-Child-Care_FINAL.pdf.

19. First Five Years Fund, "NEW POLLING: Voters, Small Businesses Agree Child Care is an Economic Imperative, Congress Must Act," November 30, 2022, https://www.ffyf.org/2022/11/30/new-polling-voters-small-businesses-agree-child-care-is-an-economic-imperative-congress-must-act/.

20. Claire Cain Miller, "How Other Nations Pay for Child Care: The U.S. Is an Outlier," *Seattle Times*, October 6, 2021, https://www.seattletimes.com/nation-world/how-other-nations-pay-for-child-care-the-u-s-is-an-outlier/.

21. White House, "Fact Sheet: Vice President Harris Announces Action to Lower Child Care Costs for More Than 100,000 Families," February 29, 2024, https://bidenwhitehouse.archives.gov/briefing-room/statements-releases/2024/02/29/fact-sheet-vice-president-harris-announces-action-to-lower-child-care-costs-for-more-than-100000-families/.

22. Ayesha Islam, Autumn R. Green, and Theresa Anderson, "The Child Care Access Means Parents in School Program (CCAMPIS)," Urban Institute, December 2022, https://www.urban.org/sites/default/files/2022–12/SPFATC-The%20Child%20Care%20Access%20Means%20Parents%20in%20School%20Program%20%28CCAMPIS%29.pdf.

23. Wonderschool, "Center-Based vs. In-Home Daycare: Finding the Best Choice for Your Child," https://www.wonderschool.com/p/child-care-provider-resources/center-based-or-in-home-childcare-what-is-best-for-your-child/, accessed April 7, 2025.

24. Administration for Children and Families, "National Survey of Early Care and Education," https://acf.gov/opre/project/national-survey-early-care-and-education, accessed April 7, 2025.

25. Administration for Children and Families, "National Survey of Early Care and Education."

26. "Head Start Program Facts Fiscal Year 2016," https://headstart.gov/sites/default/files/pdf/hs-program-fact-sheet-2016.pdf?redirect=eclkc, accessed April 7, 2025.

27. US Government Accountability Office, *Child Care: Federal Support for CCAMPIS and Head Start Programs*, GAO-24–106077, February 27, 2024, https://www.gao.gov/products/gao-24–106077.

28. Deborah Phillips, William Gormley, and Sara Anderson, "The Effects of Tulsa's CAP Head Start Program on Middle-School Academic Outcomes and Progress," *Developmental Psychology*, 2016. https://georgetown.app.box.com/s/q43pgptmzzm6h3zjcosk93ucnh1k409e.

29. Lauren Bauer and Diane Whitmore Schanzenbach, "The Long-Term Impact of the Head Start Program," Hamilton Project, August 19, 2016, https://www.hamiltonproject.org/publication/paper/the-long-term-impact-of-the-head-start-program/.

30. NHSA, "Head Start Advantage: Child Welfare," https://nhsa.org/resource/head-start-advantage-child-welfare/, accessed April 7, 2025.

CHAPTER 6: TRANSPORTATION AND WHAT FOLLOWS

1. Terry Gross, "A Forgotten History of How the U.S. Government Segregated America," NPR, May 3, 2017, https://www.npr.org/2017/05/03/526655831/a-forgotten-history-of-how-the-u-s-government-segregated-america.

2. David R. Henderson, "The Color of Law," CATO Institute (Fall 2017), https://www.cato.org/regulation/fall-2017/color-law.

3. Alex Woodward, "How Redlining Shaped New Orleans Neighborhoods: Is It Too Late to Be Fixed?" *The Gambit*, January 21, 2019, https://www.nola.com/gambit/news/how-redlining-shaped-new-orleans-neighborhoods-is-it-too-late-to-be-fixed/article_215014ce-0c15–5917-b773–8d1d2fdaa655.html.

4. Helen C. S. Meier and Bruce C. Mitchell, "Tracing the Legacy of Redlining: A New Method for Tracking the Origins of Housing Segregation," National Community Reinvestment Coalition, February 2022, https://www.ncrc.org/redlining-score/.

5. Ta-Nehisi Coates, "The Case for Reparations," *The Atlantic*, June 2014, https://www.theatlantic.com/magazine/archive/2014/06/the-case-for-reparations/361631/.

6. "Mapping Inequality: Redlining in New Deal America," University of Richmond, https://dsl.richmond.edu/panorama/redlining/map/OH/Cleveland/area_descriptions/D21#loc=12/41.498/-81.769&mapview=polygons, accessed April 7, 2025.

7. Diego Mendez-Carbajo, "Neighborhood Redlining, Racial Segregation, and Homeownership," *Page One Economics Newsletter*, Federal Reserve Bank of St. Louis, September 2021, https://ideas.repec.org/a/fip/fedlpo/93180.html.

8. Tracy Jan, "Redlining Was Banned 50 Years Ago. It's Still Hurting Minorities Today," *Washington Post*, March 28, 2018, https://www.washingtonpost.com/news/wonk/wp/2018/03/28/redlining-was-banned-50-years-ago-its-still-hurting-minorities-today/.

9. Newport News (Virginia), "Statistical Profile Reports," https://www.nnva.gov/1811/Statistical-Profile-Reports, accessed April 7, 2025.

10. Joint Legislative Audit and Review Commission (JLARC), *Virginia Compared with the Other States*, 2023, https://jlarc.virginia.gov/pdfs/reports/Virginia%20Compared%202023-FULL%20REPORT-FINAL.pdf.

11. US Census Bureau, "Income, Poverty, and Health Insurance Coverage in the United States: 2022," press release, September 12, 2023, https://www.census.gov/newsroom/press-releases/2023/income-poverty-health-insurance-coverage.html.

12. US Census Bureau, "QuickFacts: Macon-Bibb County, Georgia; Peachtree City, Georgia," https://www.census.gov/quickfacts/fact/table/maconbibbcountygeorgia,peachtreecitycitygeorgia/INC110219, accessed April 7, 2025.

13. Latetia V. Moore, Ana V. Diez Roux, Kelly R. Evenson, Aileen P. McGinn, and Shannon J. Brines, "Availability of Recreational Resources in Minority and Low Socioeconomic Status Areas," *American Journal of Preventive Medicine* (February 25, 2008), https://www.ncbi.nlm.nih.gov/pmc/articles/PMC2254179/.

14. T. L. McKenzie, J. S. Moody, J. A. Carlson, N. V. Lopez, and J. P. Elder, "Neighborhood Income Matters: Disparities in Community Recreation Facilities, Amenities, and Programs," *Journal of Park and Recreation Administration* 31, no. 4 (2013), https://headwaterseconomics.org/trail/123-ca-income-parks-kids-use/.

15. Ronda Chapman, Sadiya Muqueeth, Brendan Shane, Linda Hwang, and Jessica Sargent, *Parks and an Equitable Recovery* (San Francisco: Trust for Public Land, 2021), https://www.tpl.org/parks-and-an-equitable-recovery-parkscore-report.

16. Sherri Williams, "Book Deserts Leave Low-Income Neighborhoods Thirsty for Reading Material," NBC News, December 29, 2017, https://www.nbcnews.com/news/nbcblk/book-deserts-leave-low-income-neighborhoods-thirsty-reading-material-n833356.

17. Charles Lewis Nier III, "The Shadow of Credit: The Historical Origins of Racial Predatory Lending and Its Impact Upon African American Wealth Accumulation," *University of Pennsylvania Journal of Law and Social Change* 11 (2008): 131, https://archive.law.upenn.edu/journals/jlasc/articles/volume11/issue2/Nier11U.Pa.J.L.&Soc.Change131%282007%29.pdf.

18. FHWA, "NHTS BRIEF 2014—Mobility Challenges for Households in Poverty," October 22, 2014, https://nhts.ornl.gov/briefs/PovertyBrief.pdf.

19. Rebecca E. Lee, Yeonwoo Kim, and Catherine Cubbin, "Residence in Unsafe Neighborhoods Is Associated with Active Transportation Among Poor Women: Geographic Research on Wellbeing (GROW) Study," *Journal of Transport & Health* 9 (June 2018): 64–72, https://www.sciencedirect.com/science/article/abs/pii/S2214140517307211, https://www.sciencedirect.com/science/article/abs/pii/S2214140517307211.

20. Prosperity Now, *The Racial Wealth Divide in New Orleans*, https://edit.prosperitynow.org/files/resources/Racial_Wealth_Divide_in_New_Orleans_OptimizedforScreenReaders.pdf, accessed May 7, 2025.

21. Alexandra Murphy and Natasha Pilkauskas, "U-M Study Finds 1 in 4 Adults Experience Transportation Insecurity," press release, University of Michigan, September 29, 2022, https://fordschool.umich.edu/news/2022/u-m-study-finds-1-4-adults-experience-transportation-insecurity.

22. Amy E. Ng, David Adjaye-Gbewonyo, and Jennifer Dahlhamer, "Lack of Reliable Transportation for Daily Living Among Adults: United States, 2022," National Center for Health Statistics Data Brief, No. 490, 2024, https://www.cdc.gov/nchs/products/databriefs/db490.htm.

23. Sicheng Wang and Yanfeng Xu, "Transit Use for Single-Parent Households: Evidence from Maryland," *Transportation Research Interdisciplinary Perspectives* 8 (November 2020): 100223, https://www.sciencedirect.com/science/article/pii/S2590198220301342.

24. Jeff Davis, "Explainer: What the 80/20 Highway-Transit Split Really Is (and What It Isn't)," Eno Center for Transportation, July 26, 2021, https://enotrans.org/article/explainer-what-the-80-20-highway-transit-split-really-is-and-what-it-isnt/.

25. "Washington, DC Research Facts and Visitor Research," Washington DC (website), https://washington.org/research, accessed April 7, 2025.

26. Alexander Din, "Increased Transit Delays in Fall of 2021 and the Potential Impact on High School Commutes," DC Policy Center, November 14, 2022, https://www.dcpolicycenter.org/publications/metro-delays-high-school-commutes/.

27. Ian Cropper, "DART'S Fundamental Inadequacies Fail the People of Dallas," *North Texas Daily*, November 17, 2023, https://www.ntdaily.com/opinion/dart-s-fundamental-inadequacies-fail-the-people-of-dallas/article_9d58e94a-8344-11ee-85c4-27409d6d36af.html.

28. US Census Bureau, "Table 1. Household Net Worth by Race and Hispanic Origin of Householder: 2019," https://www.census.gov/data/tables/2019/demo/wealth/wealth-asset-ownership.html, accessed April 7, 2025.

29. Bureau of Transportation Statistics, "The Household Cost of Transportation: Is it Affordable?" September 19, 2023, https://www.bts.gov/data-spotlight/household-cost-transportation-it-affordable.

30. Basav Sen, "How the U.S. Transportation System Fuels Inequality," Inequality.org, January 27, 2022, https://inequality.org/research/public-transit-inequality/.

31. Alissa Walker, "Study: Lyft and Uber Drivers Discriminate Against People of Color," *Curbed*, July 2, 2018, https://archive.curbed.com/2018/7/2/17511530/lyft-ride-hailing-taxis-discrimination.

32. Ruth Steinhardt, "Rideshare Users Pay More in Low-Income and Minority Neighborhoods," *GW Today*, July 7, 2020, https://gwtoday.gwu.edu/rideshare-users-pay-more-low-income-and-minority-neighborhoods.

33. Barbara Jacoby, "What About the Other 85 Percent?" *Inside Higher Ed*, July 22, 2020, https://www.insidehighered.com/views/2020/07/23/colleges-should-be-planning-more-intentionally-students-who-commute-campuses-fall.

34. Morgan Taylor and Jonathan M. Turk, "Race and Ethnicity in Higher Education: A Look at Low-Income Undergraduates," American Council on Education, 2019, https://www.equityinhighered.org/resources/ideas-and-insights/race-and-ethnicity-in-higher-education-a-look-at-low-income-undergraduates/.

35. Sancia Celestin, "3 Ways Education Deserts Compound College Access Issues for Low Income Students," National College Attainment Network (NCAN), June 13, 2019, https://www.ncan.org/news/455779/3-Ways-Education-Deserts-Compound-College-Access-Issues-for-Low-Income-Students.htm.

36. Elaine S. Povich, "One Big Barrier for Community College Students: Transportation to Campus," *The 74 Million*, November 23, 2022, https://www.the74million.org/article/lack-of-transportation-hinders-community-college-students/.

37. Ariel Gilreath, "Transit for Toddlers: More Bus Stops Needed Near Head Start Centers," *Hechinger Report*, November 2, 2023, https://hechingerreport.org/transit-for-toddlers-more-bus-stops-needed-near-head-start-centers/.

38. Greg Garrison, "Transportation Secretary Announces $1 Billion to Reunite Communities," AL.com, June 30, 2022, https://www.al.com/news/2022/06/transportation-secretary-announces-1-billion-to-reunite-communities.

39. Cheryl Strayed, *Brave Enough: A Collection of Inspirational Quotes* (New York: Knopf, 2015).

40. Kathryn Zickuhr, "Discriminatory Housing Practices in the District: A Brief History," DC Policy Center, October 24, 2018, https://www.dcpolicycenter.org/publications/discriminatory-housing-practices-in-the-district-a-brief-history/.

41. Isabel Wilkerson, *The Warmth of Other Suns: The Epic Story of America's Great Migration*, reprint ed. (New York: Vintage, 2011).

CHAPTER 7: FOOD AND THE ORDER OF THINGS

1. Dave Roos, "How the Erie Canal Was Built with Raw Labor and Amateur Engineering," History.com, April 7, 2021, https://www.history.com/news/erie-canal-construction-engineering-labor.

2. "Statistical Reports and Tables," Virginia Department of Health, https://apps.vdh.virginia.gov/HealthStats/stats.htm?utm_source=chatgpt.com, accessed April 7, 2025.

3. "Chef José Andrés: A World-Class Chef Brings His Message to Lancaster," *Lancaster County Magazine*, November 2019, https://www.lancastercountymag.com/chef-jose-andres/.

4. Lily Melendez, "A Feast of Reciprocity: Language, Food, and Sovereignty in Indigenous Communities," Richardson Bay Audubon Center & Sanctuary, November 21, 2023, https://richardsonbay.audubon.org/news/feast-reciprocity-language-food-and-sovereignty-indigenous-communities.

5. "Connecting Cultures, Building Community Through Food," Henrico County Public Library, July 19, 2023, https://www.henricolibrary.org/news/library-news/entry/news-and-events/2023/07/19/connecting-cultures-building-community-through-food.

6. John Reardon, "Food Is Symbolic of Love When Words Are Inadequate," *Saratoga Today*, September 30, 2022, https://saratogatodaynewspaper.com/food-is-symbolic-of-love-when-words-are-inadequate-alan-d-wolfelt/.

7. "Best Of: Michael Twitty's 'Koshersoul,'" NPR, September 11, 2022, https://www.npr.org/2022/09/11/1122268631/best-of-michael-twittys-koshersoul.

8. Rachel Jewkes, Esnat Chirwa, Deda Ogum Alangea, and Adolphina Addo-Lartey, "Pooled Analysis of the Association Between Food Insecurity and Violence Against Women: Evidence from Low- and Middle-Income Settings," *Journal of Global Health* (March 2023), https://pmc.ncbi.nlm.nih.gov/articles/PMC9999307/.

9. Jin Huang, Karen M. Matta Oshima, and Youngmi Kim, "Does Food Insecurity Affect Parental Characteristics and Child Behavior? Testing Mediation Effects," *Social Service Review*, 2010, https://pmc.ncbi.nlm.nih.gov/articles/PMC4071141/.

10. Chelsea R. Singleton, "Exploring the Interconnectedness of Crime and Nutrition: Current Evidence and Recommendations to Advance Nutrition Equity Research," *Journal of the Academy of Nutrition and Dietetics* (October 2024), https://www.sciencedirect.com/science/article/pii/S2212267224001242.

11. Lee Smith, Jae Il Shin, Christina Carmichael, and Louis Jacob, "Association of Food Insecurity with Suicidal Ideation and Suicide Attempts in Adults Aged ≥50 Years from Low- and Middle-Income Countries," *Journal of Affective Disorders* (July 2022), https://pubmed.ncbi.nlm.nih.gov/35461821/.

12. Feeding America, "Feeding America Poll Shows Majority of Likely Voters Want Government to Do More to Address Food Insecurity," November 1, 2023, https://www.feedingamerica.org/about-us/press-room/farm-bill-poll.

13. Action Against Hunger, "86 Percent of Americans Say Global Hunger Remains a Serious Problem," press release, October 15, 2021, https://www.actionagainsthunger.org/press-releases/86-percent-americans-say-global-hunger-remains-serious-problem/.

14. Matthew P. Rabbitt, Laura J. Hales, Michael P. Burke, and Alisha Coleman-Jensen, *Household Food Security in the United States in 2022*, (Washington, DC: US Department of Agriculture, Economic Research Service, 2023), https://www.ers.usda.gov/webdocs/publications/107703/err-325.pdf?v=7823.1.

15. Move For Hunger, "US Food Insecurity Soars, Leaving 44 Million Americans Without Access to Food," November 14, 2023, https://moveforhunger.org/blog/us-food-insecurity-soars-leaving-44-million-americans-without-access-food.

16. WhyHunger, "Just the Facts: Hunger and Poverty in the U.S. and Globally," https://whyhunger.org/just-the-facts/, accessed April 7, 2025.

17. Feeding America, "Hunger in America," https://www.feedingamerica.org/hunger-in-america, accessed April 7, 2025.

18. No Kid Hungry, "Facts About Child Hunger in America," https://www.nokidhungry.org/who-we-are/hunger-facts, accessed April 7, 2025.

19. Laura J. Hales, "More Than Half of All Food-Insecure Households Work Full Time," US Department of Agriculture, Economic Research Service, December 7, 2023, https://www.ers.usda.gov/data-products/chart-gallery/gallery/chart-detail/?chartId=108053.

20. Alisha Coleman-Jensen, "Food Insecurity More Common for Households with Nonstandard Work Arrangements," US Department of Agriculture, Economic Research Service, June 5, 2012, https://www.ers.usda.gov/amber-waves/2012/june/food-insecurity.

21. No Kid Hungry, "Facts About Child Hunger in America."

22. Feeding America, "Facts About Senior Hunger," https://www.feedingamerica.org/hunger-in-america/senior-hunger-facts, accessed April 7, 2025.

23. Tara O'Neill Hayes, "Food Insecurity and Food Insufficiency: Assessing Causes and Historical Trends," American Action Forum, March 4, 2021, https://www.americanactionforum.org/research/food-insecurity-and-food-insufficiency-assessing-causes-and-historical-trends/.

24. *Freedom from Hunger: An Achievable Goal for the United States of America*, National Commission on Hunger, 2015, https://drexel.edu/hunger-free-center/research/briefs-and-reports/hunger-commission/root-causes/.

25. Feeding America, "Map the Meal Gap 2024: Overall Executive Summary," May 14, 2024, https://www.feedingamerica.org/research/map-the-meal-gap/overall-executive-summary.

26. Feeding America, "Food Insecurity Among the Latino Population in District of Columbia," https://map.feedingamerica.org/county/2022/hispanic/district-of-columbia, accessed April 7, 2025.

27. Feeding America, "Facts About Hunger in Black Communities," https://www.feedingamerica.org/hunger-in-america/black-communities, accessed April 7, 2025.

28. Feeding America, "New Study From Feeding America Shows Extensive Disparities in Food Insecurity at the County Level," PR Newswire, July 20, 2022, https://www.prnewswire.com/news-releases/new-study-from-feeding-america-shows-extensive-disparities-in-food-insecurity-at-the-county-level-301590344.html.

29. Aliss Higham, "Map Shows States with Highest Food Insecurity as 47 Million Go Hungry," *Newsweek*, September 5, 2024, https://www.newsweek.com/map-states-highest-food-insecurity-usda-1949122.

30. Michael W. Twitty, *The Cooking Gene: A Journey Through African American Culinary History in the Old South* (New York: Amistad, 2017).

31. Butler Center for Arkansas Studies, "Prelude to War," http://bc-digital.org/civilwararkansas/history.html, accessed April 7, 2025.

32. "Slavery," Encyclopedia of Arkansas, https://encyclopediaofarkansas.net/entries/slavery-1275/, accessed April 7, 2025.

33. "African Americans," *Encyclopedia of Arkansas*, https://encyclopediaofarkansas.net/entries/african-americans-407/, accessed April 7, 2025.

34. Mary Hennigan, "Food Insecurity in Arkansas Worsens; Rate Ranks Second Highest Nationwide," *Arkansas Advocate*, June 3, 2024, https://arkansasadvocate.com/2024/06/03/food-insecurity-in-arkansas-worsens-rate-ranks-second-highest-nationwide/.

35. "Food," George Washington's Mount Vernon, https://www.mountvernon.org/george-washington/slavery/food, accessed April 7, 2025.

36. "Forced Removal of Native Americans," Equal Justice Initiative, July 1, 2016, https://eji.org/news/history-racial-injustice-forced-removal-native-americans/.

37. Move For Hunger, "Native Americans and Food Insecurity," https://moveforhunger.org/native-americans-food-insecure, accessed April 7, 2025.

38. Move For Hunger, "Native Americans and Food Insecurity."

39. Danielle Douglas-Gabriel, "Fathers or Students: Black Men in College Often Face a Choice," *Washington Post*, February 20, 2022, https://www.washingtonpost.com/education/2022/02/20/black-fathers-in-college/.

40. Joel Berg and Angelica Gibson, "Why the World Should Not Follow the Failed United States Model of Fighting Domestic Hunger," *International Journal of Environmental Research and Public Health* (2022), https://pubmed.ncbi.nlm.nih.gov/35055636/.

41. Benedict Vigers, "U.S.: Leader or Loser in the G7?" Gallup, April 17, 2024, https://news.gallup.com/poll/643598/leader-loser.aspx.

42. "Nelson Mandela Day 2021," Unifor, July 16, 2021, https://www.unifor.org/news/all-news/nelson-mandela-day-2021.

43. Mark Nord, *Food Insecurity in Households with Children*, Economic Information Bulletin No. 56 (Washington, DC: US Department of Agriculture, Economic Research Service, 2009), https://files.eric.ed.gov/fulltext/ED508211.pdf.

44. National Center for Education Statistics, "National Postsecondary Student Aid Study (NPSAS)," US Department of Education, Institute of Education Sciences, https://nces.ed.gov/surveys/npsas/, accessed April 7, 2025.

45. Bryce McKibben, Jiayao Wu, and Sara Abelson, "New Federal Data Confirm that College Students Face Significant—and Unacceptable—Basic Needs Insecurity," HOPE Center for College, Community, and Justice, Temple University, August 3, 2023, https://hope.temple.edu/npsas.

46. Sara Goldrick-Rab, Carrie R. Welton, and Vanessa Coca, *Parenting While in College: Understanding the Challenges and Opportunities for Student Parents*, Hope Foundation, May 2020, https://www.luminafoundation.org/wp-content/uploads/2020/06/parenting-while-in-college.pdf.

47. Maya E. Maroto, Anastasia Snelling, and Henry Linck, "Food Insecurity Among Community College Students: Prevalence and Association with Grade Point Average," *Community College Journal of Research and Practice* (October 1, 2014), https://www.tandfonline.com/doi/abs/10.1080/10668926.2013.850758.

48. Aseel El Zein, Karla P. Shelnutt, Sarah Colby, and Melissa J. Vilaro, "Prevalence and Correlates of Food Insecurity Among U.S. College Students: A Multi-Institutional Study," *BMC Public Health* (May 2019), https://pmc.ncbi.nlm.nih.gov/articles/PMC6542079/.

49. James Dubick, Brandon Mathews, and Clare Cady, *Hunger on Campus: The Challenge of Food Insecurity for College Students* (Philadelphia: National Student Campaign Against Hunger and Homelessness and the College and University Food Bank

Alliance, 2016), https://studentsagainsthunger.org/wp-content/uploads/2016/10/Hunger_On_Campus.pdf.

50. Erica Phillips, Anne McDaniel, and Alicia Croft, "Food Insecurity and Academic Disruption Among College Students," *Journal of Student Affairs Research and Practice* 55, no. 4 (2018): 353–72, https://doi.org/10.1080/19496591.2018.1470003.

51. Rebecca L. Hagedorn-Hatfield, Lanae B. Hood, and Adam Hege, "A Decade of College Student Hunger: What We Know and Where We Need to Go," *Frontiers in Public Health* 10 (February 2022): 83772, https://pmc.ncbi.nlm.nih.gov/articles/PMC8913502/.

52. Julia A. Wolfson, Noura Insolera, Alicia Cohen, and Cindy W. Leung, "The Effect of Food Insecurity During College on Graduation and Type of Degree Attained: Evidence from a Nationally Representative Longitudinal Survey," *Public Health Nutrition* 25, no. 2 (February 2022): 389–97, https://doi.org/10.1017/S1368980021003104.

53. Kalee Burns, Liana Fox, and Danielle Wilson, "Expansions to Child Tax Credit Contributed to 46% Decline in Child Poverty Since 2020," US Census Bureau, September 13, 2022, https://www.census.gov/library/stories/2022/09/record-drop-in-child-poverty.html.

54. Paul R. Shafer, Katherine M. Gutiérrez, Stephanie Ettinger de Cuba, and Allison Bovell-Ammon, *Association of the Implementation of Child Tax Credit Advance Payments with Food Insufficiency in US Households*, Children's HealthWatch, January 13, 2022, https://childrenshealthwatch.org/wp-content/uploads/shafer_2022_oi_211202_1641586727.69679.pdf.

55. Spencer Kimball, "Child Poverty More Than Doubled in U.S. After Expanded Tax Credits, Stimulus Checks Ended," CNBC, September 12, 2023, https://www.cnbc.com/2023/09/12/child-poverty-surged-after-stimulus-checks-tax-credits-ended.html.

56. Chabeli Carrazana, "A Bigger Child Tax Credit Isn't Coming. The Senate Just Voted Against It," *The 19th*, August 1, 2024, https://19thnews.org/2024/08/child-tax-credit-2024-senate-votes-against-bill/.

57. Center on Budget and Policy Priorities, "A Quick Guide to SNAP Eligibility and Benefits," September 30, 2024, https://www.cbpp.org/research/food-assistance/a-quick-guide-to-snap-eligibility-and-benefits.

58. US Department of Agriculture, Food and Nutrition Service, "National and State Level Estimates of WIC Eligibility and Program Reach in 2021," https://www.fns.usda.gov/research/wic/eligibility-and-program-reach-estimates-2021, accessed April 7, 2025.

59. Wendy Lopez, "There's Still So Much Stigma About SNAP. Here's What Needs to Change," *Self*, April 2, 2021, https://www.self.com/story/barriers-and-stigma-facing-snap.

60. Allison Y. Zhu, "Impact of Neighborhood Sociodemographic Characteristics on Food Store Accessibility in the United States Based on the 2020 US Census Data," *Delaware Journal of Public Health* 8, no. 3 (August 2022): 94–101, https://pmc.ncbi.nlm.nih.gov/articles/PMC9495479/.

61. Zhu, "Impact of Neighborhood Sociodemographic Characteristics on Food Store Accessibility in the United States Based on the 2020 US Census Data," 94–101.

62. Colleen Curtis, "First Lady Michelle Obama on Making a Difference in Cities with Food Deserts," *The White House Blog*, October 25, 2011, https://obama whitehouse.archives.gov/blog/2011/10/25/first-lady-michelle-obama-making -difference-cities-food-deserts.

63. News and Notes, "The Kitchen of a Civil Rights Hero," NPR, July 4, 2005, https://www.npr.org/2005/07/04/4728761/the-kitchen-of-a-civil-rights-hero.

CHAPTER 8: HOUSING AND BEGINNINGS

1. Madeleine McQuilling, "Robert Taylor Homes," Hal Baron Project, University of Illinois at Urbana-Champaign, updated April 14, 2022, https://halbaronproject.web .illinois.edu/omeka/items/show/44.

2. Madeleine Parrish and Chima Ikoro, "Chicago Public Schools and Segregation," Firsthand: Segregation, https://www.wttw.com/firsthand/segregation/chicago -public-schools-and-segregation, accessed April 7, 2025.

3. Chelsea Birchmier, "The Negro Worker in the Chicago Labor Market: A Case Study of De Facto Segregation (Harold M. Baron and Bennett Hymer, 1965)," Hal Baron Project, June 26, 2020, https://publish.illinois.edu/halbaronproject/2020/06/26 /the-negro-worker-in-the-chicago-labor-market-a-case-study-of-de-facto-segregation -harold-m-baron-and-bennett-hymer-1965/.

4. David Wilson, *Inventing Black-on-Black Violence: Discourse, Space, and Representation* (Syracuse, NY: Syracuse University Press, 2005).

5. Erik Gellman, "Robert Taylor Homes," *Encyclopedia of Chicago*, http://www .encyclopedia.chicagohistory.org/pages/2478.html, accessed April 7, 2025.

6. Jacqueline Serrato, "Growing Up in the Robert Taylor Housing Projects," *South Side Weekly*, February 25, 2022, https://southsideweekly.com/growing-up-in -the-robert-taylor-housing-projects/.

7. Roberta G. Reid with Martha W. McCartney, *Reconnaissance Survey of Historic Architecture, Newport News, Virginia*, September 1990, https://www.dhr.virginia.gov/pdf_files /SpecialCollections/NN-030_Recon_Survey_Historic_AH_Newport_News_1990 _DHR_report.pdf.

8. Allison Bazzle, "Tenants in Newport News Given 30-Day Notice to Vacate Apartments After New Company Buys Complex," 13News Now, January 11, 2023, https://www.13newsnow.com/article/news/local/mycity/newport-news/tenants -newport-news-virginia-given-30-day-notice-to-vacate-apartments/291–540f87f0 –857f-4c95-a2f2–877fc450e0f1.

9. Ryan Murphy, "Hampton Roads' Cities Still Have Some of the HIGHEST EVICTION RATES in the Country, New Analysis Finds," WHRO, January 8, 2025, https://www.whro.org/business-growth/2025–01–08/hampton-roads-cities-still-have -some-of-the-highest-eviction-rates-in-the-country-new-analysis-finds.

10. US Census Bureau, "Nearly Half of Renter Households Are Cost Burdened, Proportions Differ by Race," press release, September 12, 2024, https://www.census .gov/newsroom/press-releases/2024/renter-households-cost-burdened-race.html.

11. Claire Zippel, "A Broken Foundation: Affordable Housing Crisis Threatens DC's Lowest-Income Residents," DC Fiscal Policy Institute, December 8, 2016, https://www.dcfpi.org/all/a-broken-foundation-affordable-housing-crisis-threatens -dcs-lowest-income-residents-2/.

12. National Low Income Housing Coalition, "The Problem," https://nlihc.org/explore-issues/why-we-care/problem, accessed April 9, 2025.

13. National Low Income Housing Coalition, "California," https://nlihc.org/oor/state/ca, accessed April 9, 2025.

14. Whitney Airgood-Obrycki, "Rental Housing Unaffordability: How Did We Get Here?" Joint Center for Housing Studies of Harvard University, March 26, 2024, https://www.jchs.harvard.edu/blog/rental-housing-unaffordability-how-did-we-get-here.

15. "History of U.S. Homeownership: How Housing Has Changed Since 1960," *The Zebra*, March 13, 2024, https://www.thezebra.com/resources/home/housing-trends-visualized/.

16. Juliana Menasce Horowitz, Ruth Igielnik, and Rakesh Kochhar, "Trends in Income and Wealth Inequality," Pew Research Center, January 9, 2020, https://www.pewresearch.org/social-trends/2020/01/09/trends-in-income-and-wealth-inequality/.

17. Gloria Guzman, "Median Income of Non-Hispanic White Households Increased While Asian, Black and Hispanic Median Household Income Did Not Change," US Census Bureau, September 10, 2024, https://www.census.gov/library/stories/2024/09/household-income-race-hispanic.html.

18. Lawrence Yun, Jessica Lautz, Nadia Evangelou, and Brandi Snowden, *Snapshot of Race and Home Buying in America* (Washington, DC: National Association of Realtors, 2025), https://www.nar.realtor/research-and-statistics/research-reports/snapshot-of-race-and-home-buying-in-america.

19. Pew Research Center, "Where Homes Cost the Most and Where Prices Have Risen Fastest," October 25, 2024, https://www.pewresearch.org/short-reads/2024/10/25/a-look-at-the-state-of-affordable-housing-in-the-us/sr_24–10–25_housing-affordability_5/.

20. Bruce C. Mitchell, Jad Edlebi, Helen C. S. Meier, Jason Richardson, Joseph Dean, and Liang Chen, *Displaced by Design: Fifty Years of Gentrification and Black Cultural Displacement in US Cities* (Washington, DC: National Community Reinvestment Coalition, 2025), https://ncrc.org/displaced-by-design/.

21. National Women's Law Center, *Gender and Racial Justice in Housing* (Washington, DC: National Women's Law Center, 2021), https://nwlc.org/wp-content/uploads/2021/02/Gender-and-Racial-Justice-in-Housing.pdf.

22. National Women's Law Center, "NWLC Releases New Demographic Data on Rent-Burdened Single Women," press release, February 9, 2024, https://nwlc.org/press-release/nwlc-releases-new-demographic-data-on-rent-burdened-single-women/.

23. Kelly Shue and Paul Goldsmith-Pinkham, "Single Women Get Lower Returns from Housing Investments," Yale Insights, Yale School of Management, February 25, 2020, https://insights.som.yale.edu/insights/single-women-get-lower-returns-from-housing-investments.

24. John F. Kennedy, "Remarks of John F. Kennedy in a Campaign Speech on the National Housing Crisis, Boston, Massachusetts, June, 1946," John F. Kennedy Presidential Library and Museum, https://www.jfklibrary.org/archives/other-resources/john-f-kennedy-speeches/boston-ma-19460601.

25. Claudia D. Solari, "America's Housing Is Getting More Crowded. How Will That Affect Children?" Urban Wire, Urban Institute, April 24, 2019, https://www

.urban.org/urban-wire/americas-housing-getting-more-crowded-how-will-affect-children.

26. Solari, "America's Housing Is Getting More Crowded."

27. Amy Dworsky, "Voices of Youth Count: Understanding and Ending Youth Homelessness," Chapin Hall, University of Chicago, https://www.chapinhall.org/project/voices-of-youth-count/, accessed April 13, 2025.

28. Chapin Hall, *Missed Opportunities: Pregnant and Parenting Youth Experiencing Homelessness in America* (Chicago: Chapin Hall, University of Chicago, 2018), https://www.chapinhall.org/wp-content/uploads/VoYC-PP-Brief-FINAL.pdf.

29. "Forced Relocations Hit Poor Particularly Hard," Crown Family School of Social Work, Policy, and Practice, University of Chicago, SSA Magazine Archive, December 1, 2016, https://crownschool.uchicago.edu/news-events/magazine/forced-relocations-hit-poor-particularly-hard.

30. American Psychological Association, "Moving Repeatedly in Childhood Associated with Poorer Quality of Life Years Later," press release, 2010, https://www.apa.org/news/press/releases/2010/06/moving-well-being.

31. National Center for Healthy Housing, "State of Healthy Housing," https://nchh.org/tools-and-data/data/state-of-healthy-housing/, accessed April 13, 2025.

32. Sophia Wedeen, "Greater Assistance Needed to Combat the Persistence of Substandard Housing," Joint Center for Housing Studies, Harvard University, August 1, 2023, https://www.jchs.harvard.edu/blog/greater-assistance-needed-combat-persistence-substandard-housing.

33. Michael Neal, Amalie Zinn, and Linna Zhu, *Implications of Housing Conditions for Racial Wealth and Health Disparities* (Washington, DC: Urban Institute, January 2024), https://www.urban.org/sites/default/files/2024–01/Implications%20of%20Housing%20Conditions%20for%20Racial%20Wealth%20and%20Health%20Disparities_0.pdf.

34. Wedeen, "Greater Assistance Needed to Combat the Persistence of Substandard Housing."

35. National Alliance to End Homelessness, "State of Homelessness: 2024 Edition," https://endhomelessness.org/state-of-homelessness/, accessed June 27, 2025.

36. Mollie Bryant, "Homeless Shelters Don't Have Enough Beds in Many Communities," *Streetlight News*, April 29, 2024, https://streetlightnews.org/homeless-shelters/.

37. National Low Income Housing Coalition, *Impact of Hurricane Maria* (Washington, DC: National Low Income Housing Coalition, 2019), https://nlihc.org/sites/default/files/Hurricane-Impact-Maria.pdf.

38. Hope Center, *The Hope Center Survey 2021: Basic Needs Insecurity During the Ongoing Pandemic* (Philadelphia: Temple University, 2021), https://hope.temple.edu/sites/hope/files/media/document/HopeSurveyReport2021.pdf.

39. Dana Braga, "One-in-Four U.S. Parents Say They've Struggled to Afford Food or Housing in the Past Year," Pew Research Center, December 7, 2022, https://www.pewresearch.org/short-reads/2022/12/07/one-in-four-u-s-parents-say-theyve-struggled-to-afford-food-or-housing-in-the-past-year/.

40. Sara Goldrick-Rab, Carrie R. Welton, and Vanessa Coca, *Parenting While in College: Basic Needs Insecurity Among Students with Children*, Hope Center

(Philadelphia: Temple University, May 2020), https://frac.org/wp-content/uploads/2019
_ParentingStudentsReport.pdf.

41. Autumn Green, "Student Housing Is Scarce for College Students Who Have Kids," *The Conversation*, October 6, 2020, https://theconversation.com/student-housing-is-scarce-for-college-students-who-have-kids-145162.

42. Jeffrey Masters, "Ritchie Torres About to Make LGBTQ History in Congress," *The Advocate*, October 7, 2020, https://www.advocate.com/politics/2020/10/07/ritchie-torres-about-make-lgbtq-history-congress.

43. David Saxon, "In Praise of Lord Kelvin," *Physics World*, December 17, 2007, https://physicsworld.com/a/in-praise-of-lord-kelvin/.

44. Yuliya Panfil and Sabiha Zainulbhai, "The First Step to Solving the Housing Crisis Might Be Simpler Than You Think," *Politico*, May 4, 2023, https://www.politico.com/news/magazine/2023/05/04/solving-the-housing-crisis-00095075.

45. National Low Income Housing Coalition, "The Problem," https://nlihc.org/explore-issues/why-we-care/problem, accessed April 13, 2025.

46. Courtney Cooperman, "Increase Dedicated Resources for the National Housing Trust Fund," Federation of American Scientists, February 22, 2024, https://fas.org/publication/invest-in-htf/.

47. "Mayor Bowser Announces First National Housing Trust Fund Project Financed in Washington, DC," press release, DC.gov, August 7, 2019, https://mocrs.dc.gov/release/mayor-bowser-announces-first-national-housing-trust-fund-project-financed-washington-dc.

CHAPTER 9: THE SCARS AND THE DREAM

1. Briana Contreras, "Poverty Is the Fourth Leading Cause of Death in the United States, Study Finds," *Managed Healthcare Executive*, April 23, 2023, https://www.managedhealthcareexecutive.com/view/poverty-is-the-fourth-leading-cause-of-death-in-the-united-states-study-finds.

2. Children's Defense Fund, *Child Poverty: 2023 State of America's Children Report*, https://www.childrensdefense.org/tools-and-resources/the-state-of-americas-children/soac-child-poverty/, accessed April 13, 2025.

3. Alicia Garza, *The Purpose of Power: How We Come Together When We Fall Apart* (New York: One World, 2020).

4. Generation Hope, *National Student Parent Survey Results & Recommendations: Uncovering the Student Parent Experience and Its Impact on College Success* (Washington, DC: Generation Hope, 2020), https://www.generationhope.org/student-parents-report-2020.

5. Barbara Gault, Lindsey Reichlin, Elizabeth Reynolds, and Meghan Froehner, *4.8 Million College Students Are Raising Children*, Institute for Women's Policy Research (Washington, DC: Institute for Women's Policy Research, November 2014), https://www.luminafoundation.org/files/resources/college-students-raising-children.pdf.

6. "Toni Morrison on Trauma, Survival, and Finding Meaning," CTFORUM, YouTube, May 4, 2001, https://www.youtube.com/watch?v=5xvJYrSsXPA.

INDEX